Vegetarian London
Edition 2005

(MAP) indicates that you'll find a local map of the area on the page.

Credits

Design by Mickaël Charbonnel with help from Jill Spence and Alex Boylan. Cover photo by Mike Bourke.

Photos by Alex Bourke, Mike Bourke, Mickaël Charbonnel, Jennifer Wharton.

Contributors: Andrea Jenkins, Tony & Yvonne Bishop Weston, Vanessa Clarke, Kim Coussell, Peter Despard, Lesley & Paul Dove, Paul Gaynor, Sean Gifford, Dr Michael Grill, Brian Jacobs, Christine Klein, Laurence Klein, Läyne Kuirk-Schwarz-Waad, Nitin Mehta M.B.E., Sherry Nicholls, everyone at London Vegans, Claire Ranyard, Julie Rosenfield, Bani Sethi, Zofia Torun, Jennifer Wharton, Lucy Wills, Ronny Worsey, Suzanne Wright and everyone else ... THANK YOU!!!

Cataloguing in details

VEGETARIAN LONDON 2005
(5th edition) by Alex Bourke

ISBN 1-902259-05X
Published January 2005 by
Vegetarian Guides Ltd,
PO Box 2284,
London W1A 5UH, England

UK & Worldwide distribution:
Portfolio Books, Unit 5
Perivale Industrial Park
Horsenden Lane South
Greenford, Middlesex
UB6 7RL England
Tel: (+44) 020-8997 9000
Fax: (+44) 020-8997 9097
sales@portfoliobooks.com

USA and Canada book trade distributor:

Casemate
2114 Darby Road,
Havertown, PA 19083, USA
Tel: 610-853 9131
Fax: 610-853 9146
casemate@
casematepublishing.com

Vegetarian Guides available
worldwide mail order at:
www.vegetarianguides.com

Introduction

Welcome to our fifth edition! Stuffed with 400 places to eat and shop, many of them new, our latest guide is easier to use than ever. Firstly there are **more and bigger maps** with restaurant names and page numbers. Secondly **new hotspot pages**, with a purple border from top to bottom, highlight areas with a concentration of veggie delights. Thirdly there are **eight extra indexes** for cheap eats, Posh for impressing a client, vegan, organic, cafes, breakfast, child friendly, and places with alcohol.

Prices have risen in London, but **vegetarian restaurants remain terrific value.** You'll find it hard to spend as much as £30 on a three course meal with drinks at gourmet restaurants 222, Manna or The Gate, whilst the cheapest all-you-can-eat buffet at Indian Veg in Islington has actually fallen in price to £2.95.

There has been an **explosion of cafes** across the capital. All the coffee chains now offer soya milk, though Starbucks, the first to do so, continues to charge a premium. Independent cafes such as **Beatroot, Alara** and

newcomers **Pogo** and **Organic13** thrive by offering better food and more genuine service. The nine London branches of wholefood supermarkets **Fresh & Wild** and **Planet Organic** also now have bustling cafe and juice areas.

As Atkins fades into last year's fad, the hot new **low glycaemic index (G.I.) lifetime diet** emphasises unrefined carbohydrates, beans, nuts, veg and fruit, in other words a wholefood vegetarian, or rather vegan, diet. You'll find such nutrient dense, calorie low, delicious food throughout this guide.

Whether you're veggie, vegan, meat reducing, or just seeking the highest quality food at a fair price, this is your best guide ever... until 2006! Happy scoffing!

Alex Bourke

Our Top 5 Best of London

With over 100 vegetarian restaurants and cafes in London, it's hard to know where to start. Here are some suggestions.

Take away lunch

Carrie Awaze
Health Food Centre
Pure
Red Veg
Spitalfields Market

Healthiest

222
Country Life
Fresh & Wild
Planet Organic
VitaOrganic

Lively night out

Eat & Two Veg
Mildred's
Tai (then the West End)
Tea Room des Artistes
Wagamama

New places

222
Chandni
Eat & Two Veg
Organic13
Pogo Cafe

Community feel

Alara
Bonnington Cafe
Bumblebee Wholefoods
Neal's Yard Bakery
Pogo Cafe

Innovative

Little Earth Cafe
Neal's Yard Salad Bar
Organic13
Peking Palace
Tiffin Bites

Desserts & Cakes

Beatroot
Higher Taste
Mildred's
Pogo Cafe
Riverside Vegetaria

What's Hot in the Stores

by Tony Bishop-Weston

Londoner Tony Bishop-Weston, foodie and co-author of a new vegan cookbook by Hamlyn, sniffs out what's new on the shelves in the shops.

It's like they all just suddenly woke up and smelt the vegan coffee – maybe it's the lure of the green pound, but all of a sudden we seem awash with vegan deliciousness, hummus wraps and soyaccinos. Never mind the salubrious Planet Organic and Fresh and Wild, even Selfridges' food hall has more than a hamper-full of vegan goodies – with more nuts, seeds and dairy free live yoghurts than Gillian McKeith can shake a stick at. Here are my favourite top 10 new items for this year.

Heaven on toast!

Top place has to go to **Redwood's new melting "cheese"** – a fantasy come true for me. Opening the door to a full dairy-free experience at Pizza Express, who are currently trialing this product, will ensure Redwoods a big place in the vegan history books. Combined with the new (fairly unhealthy) delicious and frighteningly realistic veggie burger from Wicken Fen, some Dijon mustard, the new Nomato ketchup or Plamil mayonnaise, and a jungle of greenery, this facilitated munching the best two cheese burgers I have ever had the pleasure to be guilty of eating.

Tiger in your Tank

Bottle Green, who make **Tiger White milk** from tiger nuts, admit it takes a bit of getting used to – like Marmite, olives or tofu. The Spanish guzzle gallons of the stuff and clearly love it – putting British consumption of dairy free milks to shame. I'm a lover not hater and thought it tasted a bit like goat's milk. I'm eager to try to make some Tiger White cheese, it might sway my veggie missus.

Making Waves

Redwood's fish alternatives are amazing and will help a lot of people struggling to think of more high protein snacks. The **Making Waves** range epitomises veganism's bigger solution for me – the chance to deliciously benefit people, animals and the environment. Scampi bites, tuna, salmon – don't buy them if you don't like fish – do buy them if you do and save a few.

Mr Booja Booja

The other thing we seem to be floating in a vegan sea of at the moment is dairy free chocolate. Mr **Booja Booja** is the Daddy and if you love someone a big lot then their papier mache gift boxes will ensure you more than a snog. Hot on their heels are collections of chocolates by **Montezuma**, **The Cocoa Tree**, a real cherry chocolate from **Green and Blacks** (soon to be Cadburys) and **Plamil** who also have chocolate body paint. Check out Liberty's chocolate department. Even Sainsbury's have a dairy-like chocolate, almond and soy milk bar. If you haven't discovered the **Thornton's ginger bar** yet – *get a life!* it's only 50p.

Keep Off The Grass?

If only I could convince **Plamil** to swap the omega-6 laden sunflower oil for cheap as chips omega-3 rich rapeseed oil or better still hemp-seed oil, their delicious new **mayonnaise with lemongrass** would be as good as it

Booja Booja

tastes. Mixed with some capers, sundried tomato pesto and a sprinkle of nori seaweed flakes, this is divine with Redwood's vegan scampi. My 80:20 rule nutritionist wife, being half Dutch, prefers to dunk her chips in it.

Champagne Charlies

What a game we had trying to find **affordable wine** for our wedding. Thank goodness for the **Co-Op** and their honest labelling policy which seems to have sparked many others into action. **Tesco** have started to mark wine on their shelves but you're still not sure if it's vegan or just vegetarian. **Oddbins** are great bless

...What's Hot in the Stores

them and **Vinceremos** are committed to a comprehensive relabelling. Look out for new wines from **Carmel** and also some of the **English Vineyards**, who are starting to give the French a run for their money as global warming levels the playing field. And don't miss the **Vintage Roots** mail order catalogue of vegetarian and vegan wines. **(see page 3)**

Cinderella? Rockafella?

There are many new companies looking to fulfill the demand for some vegan shoes that you can be seen dead in. Natalie from **Beyond Skin (see page 6)** seems to have friends in all the right places and has stubbornly

Carmel

fought to make her shoes the most ethical money can buy. Made in London (where they've never heard of the minimum wage) they don't come cheap at over £100 a pair but they are exquisite. (25% discount to Vegan Society members.)

My Mate, My Might

Vitam Yeast Extract looks more like malt extract and its taste is truly inspirational. Our office Marmite hater still hated it but he doesn't like olives either. There's an organic version and you need to tell your health food store it's available from Essential Trading in Bristol. Try in a sandwich with dairy-free cream cheese, posh lettuce and thin slices of Granny Smith apples.

Well Oil Be

I'm sure **Yaoh** (page 8) are planning to take over the world in the next few years and sort it all out. In addition to their **hemp based lotions and bath products**, Yaoh have also launched some delicious new hemp food-stuffs - **raw energy bars** and now 250 ml competitively priced **organic hemp oil**, notable for its balance of

omega oils. Yaoh have offered substantial bribes to encourage the doubling of Vegan Society members during the Diamond Jubilee year, so reward them by being healthy and clean, inside and out, Yaoh Style.

Make Up Not Break Up

There really are too many new **cosmetics** to mention, so just look for the **Vegan Society logo (page 11)** to be sure you are on the right track. **Green People** have a lot of things that others don't and are 100% organic, whilst **Tisserand** are adding to their range all the time. I love **Lush** – their shop in Carnaby Street is like Aladdin's cave – I can't help rubbing all the little bottles of potions to check for genies and *always* end up covered in Tinkerbell's fairy dust.

Remember it's your shopping basket that is your most powerful weapon to make a difference to people, animals and the environment. **www.animalfreeshopper.com** for more vegan goodies.

The Author

Tony Bishop Weston's vegan guesthouse in Scotland won the Vegetarian Hotel of the Year award in 1995. He is

Beyond Skin

the author of the ground-breaking vegan cookbook Rainbows & Wellies and *has worked for both the Vegan Society and the Vegetarian Society. He is now in partnership with his wife* **Yvonne Bishop Weston**, *who held key roles at Holland & Barrett, Cranks and cureently The Food Doctor. She now runs her own nutrition and catering consultancy www.foodsforlife.org.uk.* **The Vegan Cookbook,** *by Tony and Yvonne, £12.99, is published by Hamlyn.*

What Do You Mean, You "ONLY" Eat Fish?

Go Vegetarian!

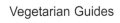 

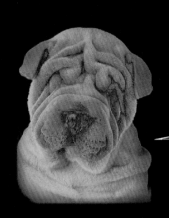

NEVER OUT OF DATE !

www.vegetarianguides.co.uk

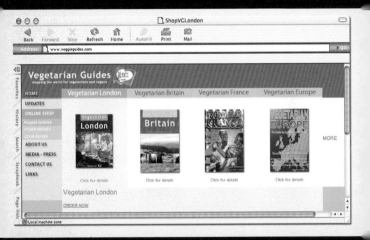

REGULAR UPDATES
www.vegetarianguides.co.uk/updates

VEGGIE NEWS
Features about veggie travel
Extracts from other Vegetarian Guides

AND A LOT MORE...
Nutrition, recipes and links to veggie websites from

CENTRAL LONDON

SOHO Central London

Soho is famous for theatres, cinema, the film industry, nightclubs and... nine veggie cafes and restaurants.

For chilling out in a cafe we love Beatroot on Berwick Street. Red Veg has the best veggie-burgers, or try Maoz falafel bar which stays open well past midnight.

For a proper sit down meal there are Mildred's, Country Life and Woodlands.

Fresh & Wild is a tremendous wholefoods supermarket on two floors with a cafe, and there are plenty more supplies and snacks at Country Life and Holland & Barrett stores.

Beatroot, one of our favourite cafes

22

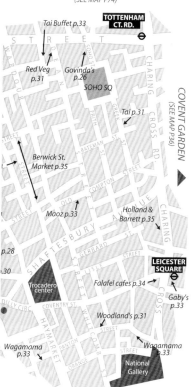

TOTTENHAM CT RD
(SEE MAP P74)

Tai Buffet p.33

TOTTENHAM CT. RD.

Red Veg p.31

Govinda's p.26

SOHO SQ

Tai p.31

COVENT GARDEN
(SEE MAP P36)

Berwick St. Market p.35

Maoz p.33

Holland & Barrett p.35

p.28

p.30

Trocadero center

Falafel cafes p.34

LEICESTER SQUARE

Woodland's p.31

Gaby's p.33

Wagamama p.33

Wagamama p.33

National Gallery

Tai Oriental vegan buffet

London has a reputation as an expensive city, but it's also home to hundreds of thousands of students who live well by knowing where to look. You could pay £40 for a theatre, the same again for dinner, and easily top £100 per head with a few drinks and a taxi home. On the other hand £10 could buy you an all you can eat buffet at Govinda's or Tai, a movie at Prince Charles Cinema, with enough left over for tomorrow's newspaper from the late night vendors by Leicester Square.

Plant at 47 Poland Street closed just as we went to press but there is a possibility of reopening in 2005. Check our website for news. (see page 19)

Beatroot

*Vegetarian
& vegan cafe*

Open:

Mon–Tue 09.00–20.30
Wed–Sat 09.00–21.00
Sun closed

Smoking allowed outside
No credit cards

92 Berwick Street, Soho
London W1V 3PP
Tel: 020–7437 8591
Tube: Oxford Circus
Tottenham Court Rd,
Piccadilly Circus
See map on page 23

Our favourite central London café, with almost all desserts vegan, near the south end of Berwick St by the fruit and veg market.

Couple of outside tables.

They do take-away too so it gets a bit manic at lunchtime, whereas in the afternoon you could sit quietly here and write a letter.

Point to whatever you fancy from 16 hot dishes and salads and they'll fill a box for you, small £3.15, medium £4.15 or large £5.15. Choose from, for example, tomato walnut and spinach pasta, spicy Moroccan tangine, organic rice, all kinds of salads. Soup with bread £2.40.

Lots of cakes, mostly vegan, £1.50–1.90 including fabulous vegan chocolate dream cake with vegan custard 50p extra, organic tofu cheesecake, vegan carrot cake, hemp flapjacks.

Fresh juices such as Vitalizer (apple, carrot, ginger), Beatnik (beetroot, carrot, celery) or Vego (celery, spinach, carrot), 8oz for £1.90 or 12oz for £2.60. "Booster" health drink (banana, spirulina and peanut butter) £1.90 or £2.40. Gorgeous soya-fruit smoothies made with orange, mango or blueberry, small £1.60, large £2.20. Teas £1.10, filter coffee £1.40.

If you like this you'll probably like the new Pogo Cafe in Hackney, East London, great for chilling out with vegan cakes and soya cappuccino.

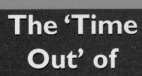

Govinda's

Vegetarian
Indian restaurant

Open:

Mon–Sat 12.00–20.00
(last orders)
Sun closed

No smoking. Children welcome.

9/10 Soho Street
Soho
London W1V 5DA
Tel: 020 020-7437-4928
Tube: Tottenham Court Rd

See map on page 23

Popular Hare Krishna owned and staffed vegetarian, Indian restaurant and café, with some fast food, next door to their temple, just off Oxford Street and near Tottenham Court Road.

No eggs, garlic or onion.

Surplus grub is given to London's homeless after hours and their Food For Life project cooks specially for them after hours.

2 vegan and 4 veggie starters such as mixed veg sabjia, pakoras or dahl with bread £2 eat in, £1.50 take-away.

Several vegan and 9 veggie choices to make your large £4.20 or regular £2.50 mixed salad.

10 main course dishes, but the best value of all is the 7 dish all-you-can-eat buffet £5.95. Happy hour 7pm–8pm £4.95.

As well as Indian food there are pizza and baked potatoes for £1.85 eat in, £1.35 take-away.

Several desserts and cakes and more of them are now vegan: apple crumble or fruitcake £1.80, muffin 80p. Energy balls 90p.

Many drinks 80p–£1.60.

Juice bar with smoothies £2.35 such as strawberry, mango, blueberry, raspberry. Soya milk sometime available. Freshly squeezed orange juice £1.50–2.35.

If you like this you may also like Indian Vegetarian Bhelpuri House in Islington for its great value buffet and vegan lassi.

Mildred's

Open:

Mon–Sat 12.30–23.00
Sun closed

Cheques & debit cards, but no credit cards.

No smoking. Children welcome.

45 Lexington Street,
Soho,
London W1

Tel: 020 7494 1634

Tube: Piccadilly Circus,
Oxford Circus

See map on page 22

Stylish vegetarian café-restaurant and take-away with hip young clientele to match, crowded and enthu-siastic. This is the top place in Soho for veggies going out for dinner and a bottle of wine. It can get quite noisy but is lots of fun.

The food is modern European with some Asian influences. Lots of healthy Mediterranean or stir-fry, but you can also have a burger and fries.

Lunchtime takeaway specials include burger of the day with salad and fries £4.70; stir-fry with rice or wheat noodles £4.20, with cashews £4.70, with tofu £5.20, with both £5.70; fried or stir-fried veg with brown rice; ener-gizing detox salad £4.40, with tofu £4.90.

Lite bites like ciabata or walnut bread.

Many of the main courses are vegan, such as stir-fried veg in soy and sesame oil with ginger on organic brown rice for £6, add organic tofu £7.50. There's also a larger detox salad with organic carrots, sprouted beans, chick peas, sultanas and toasted seeds with lemon-grass and ginger dressing for £5.50.

Several desserts include vegan chocolate and nut pudding with mocha sauce; or tofu, banana, lemon and coconut cheesecake with maple syrup and soya cream, £4.25.

Organic smoothies and juices, £2.95.

Fully licensed. Cheques and debit cards but no credit cards. Optional 12.5% service charge added to the bill.

No reservations but you can have a drink at the bar at the front while you wait.

If you like this you may also like new vegetarian restaurant and bar Eat & Two Veg in Marylebone (Central London).

Country Life

Vegan restaurant and wholefood store

Open:

Mon–Thu 11.30–21.00
Fri 11.30–14.30
Sat closed
Sun 12–18.00

No smoking. No alcohol
MC, Visa. Children welcome.

3-4 Warwick Street
near Piccadilly, London W1
Tel: 020-7434 2922
Tube: Piccadilly Circus, exit 1

See map on page 22

Herbivore heaven at this central vegan wholefood restaurant, mainly organic. 70% of the lunch trade aren't vegetarian which tells you how good it is. Now expanding, with more take-aways and a salad bar in the shop, fresh organic fruit, and organic sun-dried fruit from Cameroon.

Fabulous, delicious and extremely healthy self-serve lunchtime buffet with salad bar and hot wholefood dishes, fresh bread, £1.10 per 100 grammes. Also soups and take-aways.

In the evening the buffet is eat as much as you like for £9.50 and there is also gourmet à la carte. Soup from £2.20, starters from £2.25, main course from £7.95. Mains include Tofu Rissoles made with organic tofu, bulgar, fresh onion puree, olive oil, parsely, garlic powder and oregano; Mediterranean Courgette with organic butter beans, tomato sauce, fresh onions and basil.

Wonderful desserts from £2 are all vegan such as banana carobella, banana cinnamon cake, ice cream, lemon cheesecake.

Alcohol free wine and other non alcoholic drinks.

Wholefood shop upstairs with vegan yogurt and ice-cream, wholemeal bread and rolls, biscuits, snacks, cookbooks. Open Mon–Thu 08-18.00, Fri to 14.30, Sun 12-18.00. If you need any product not in the shop, they will get it for you.

Vegan GP for private consul-tations.

Fresh & Wild Soho

Wholefood supermarket and cafe

Open:

Mon–Fri	08.00–21.00
Sat	09.00–20.00
Sun	11.30–18.30
Bank hols	12–19.00

71-75 Brewer Street
London W1R 3SL
Tel: 020-7434 3179
Tube: Piccadilly Circus

See map on page 22

Organic wholefood super-market on two floors in the middle of Brewer Street. Downstairs are heaps of take-aways, a salad bar and juice bar/cafe with seating, organic fruit and vegeta-bles.

Upstairs is a wholefood supermarket with an expertly staffed natural remedies and bodycare section.

As you enter the store, straight ahead is the deli hot buffet counter. £1.20 per 100 grammes, e.g. veg korma, Moroccan tagine, steamed green veg, broccoli, brown rice, carrot and cardamon pilaf. Mixed leaf salad complimentary with every dish over £2.

On the right are the cafe tables, drinks, smoothies, cakes and organic bread.

To the left at the back of the store, behind the big organic fruit and veg section, is a self-serve vegan salad bar:

small box £2.25, medium £3.25, large £3.99. All ingredients are clearly marked. Prepared take-aways £3.50-4.00 include pies, wraps, riceballs, slices, exotic salads, dips.

Around the tills you'll find magazines, chocolate, flapjacks and drinks

Highlights upstairs include 30 kinds of tofu, non-dairy cheeses and yoghurts, veggie ready meals, wheat-free pasta, breakfast cereals, soya dessert, organic juices, hemp and soya ice-cream.

The health and bodycare area has herbs, aromatherapy, probiotics, flax oil, supple-ments, books (including Veggie Guides) and world music. Staff have a high level of knowledge, all of them either working as practi-tioners or well on the way to qualifying.

If you like this you'll probably like their other five stores in Old Street (City), Clapham (South), Westbourne Grove (West), Camden (North) and Stoke Newington (North).

Red Veg

Vegetarian & vegan take away

95 Dean Street, Soho W1V 5RB
Tel: 020–7437–3109
Open: *Mon–Sat:* 12–22.00
Closed Sun
Tube: Tottenham Court Road

Veggie burger and falafel bar with a few tables. The whole menu is GM free.

Veggie burger £2.85, can be made spicy with kidney beans. Chilli veg £2.80, falafel £3.55, noname nuggets £3.25.

Medium fries 95p, large £1.25, breaded mushrooms £1.55.

Coffee £1.55, cappuccino £1.75, tea £1, herbal teas £1.25. Soya milk normally available.

Tai

Chinese vegan buffet restaurant

10 Greek Street, Soho W1V 5PL
Tel: 020–7287 3730
Open: every day 12.00–23.00
Tube: Tottenham Court Rd

Vegan Chinese buffet restaurant run by a Buddhist temple. (Though they may be serving dairy ice-cream.) Incredibly popular for its amazing value, delicious food.

All you can eat buffet, as many trips as you like for £5, or £6 in the evenings and all day Sunday. Allow another £1 for drink and the same for a tip. £3 or £4 for a take-away box. Rice, spring rolls, tofu, stir-fry veg, salad, soya meats, noodles, menu changes all the time.

Unlimited Chinese tea £1, organic juices £2.50, soft drinks £1.

Cash only. Non-smoking.

Woodlands Leicester Sq

Vegetarian South Indian restaurant

37 Panton St, (off Haymarket)
London SW1Y 4EA
Open: *every day 12.00–22.45*
Tel: 020–7839 7258
Tube: Piccadilly Circus,
Leicester Square

Vegetarian Indian restaurant off the south-west corner of Leicester Square, and one of four in London.

Lunchtime all you can eat buffet on weekdays for £6.99 alongside their regular menu. For more details on the dishes please see the branch in Marylebone. (p.68)

Tai Buffet

Chinese vegan buffet restaurant

3-4 Great Chapel Street
off Oxford Street, W1

Tel: 020-7439 0383
Open: every day 12.30-21.30
Tube: Tottenham Court Rd

The latest vegan Chinese all-you-can-eat buffet restaurant, also offering amazing value at £5, or £6 evenings and Sunday. Unlimited Chinese tea £1. Cash only. Non-smoking.

Maoz

Falafel cafe, open past midnight

43 Old Compton St, Soho W1
Open: *Mon-Thu* 11.00-01.00
Fri-Sat 11.00-02.00
Sun 11.00-24.00
Tube: Leicester Square

Fantastic falafel bar like the ones in Amsterdam, at the west end of the gay zone, specialising in falafel in pitta, £3-£3.50. Self-serve salad bar with large choice of salads and tahini which you pile on top of your falafel, all of which are vegan apart from the coleslaw and mayonnaise. Eat in or take-away.

New in summer 2004 are Maoz salad meals which add fries and drinks to your falafel for £3.80 small, £4.80 large.

Fresh carrot juice £1.50. Soft drinks. Non smoking. No credit cards.

www.maozfalafel.nl

Gaby's

Omnivorous Mediterranean cafe

30 Charing Cross Rd (east side)
just below Leicester Square tube,
London WC2H 0DB

Tel: 020-7836 4233
Open: *Mon-Sat* 09.00-24.00
Sun 12.00-21.00
Tube: Leicester Square

Stacks of veggie and vegan eat-ins and take-aways for great prices compared to a restaurant in a very handy location.

Point to what you want in the deli style counter, such as stuffed aubergine or pepper £6.50, pasta with herb and tomato sauce £6.50. Excellent falafels £3.50 eat in, £3 take out. 20 salads £2-3. Fries £1.70.

All kinds of alcohol, coffee, lemon and herb tea.

Wagamama

Omnivorous Japanese restaurant

14A Irving Street
opposite Garrick Theatre
London WC1V
Tel: 020-7839 2323
Open: *Mon-Thu* 12.00-23.00
       Fri-Sat 12.00-24.00
       Sun 12.30-22.00
Tube: Leicester Square,
       Charing Cross

---

8 Norris Street, off the
Haymarket, London SW1Y 4RJ
Tel: 020-7321 2755
Open: *Mon-Sat* 12.00-23.00
       Sun 12.30-22.00
Tube: Leicester Square

10A Lexington Street
London W1R 3HS
Tel: 020-7292 0990
Open: Mon-Thu 12.00-23.00
       Fri-Sat 12.00-24.00
       Sun 12.30-22.00
Tube: Piccadilly Circus

Omnivorous fast food
Japanese noodle bar with
over nine veggie and vegan
dishes. Very busy, totally
authentic, heaps of fun.

Allow about £12-£15 for a
belt-buster, less if your're
only eating mains. Prices
start at £1.30 for miso soup
up to £6.50 for an enormous
bowl of miso ramen noodles.

See Bloomsbury, WC1 branch
for menu. (page 51)

Falafel cafes Leic Square

Omnivorous cafe

North-east corner of Leicester
Square, opposite Warner West
End cinema and Hippodrome
Open: *Every day* 24 hours
Tube: Leicester Square

Basic falafel with runny tahini
sauce. Grab one after buying
a ticket at the incredibly
cheap Prince Charles Cinema
in Leicester Place. For listings
www.princecharlescinema.
com

Eatsies

Salad bar and take-away

173 Wardour Street, W1
(corner of D'Arblay St)
Tel: 020-7434 0373
Open: *Mon-Fri* 09.00-17.00
Tube: Tottenham Court Road

Huge help yourself salad bar
for £2.75. Best of the food
11-15.00. Also filled
baguettes and bagels.

Holland & Barrett

Healthfood shop

65 Charing Cross Road
just above Leciester Square
Tel: 020 7287 3193

Open: *Mon–Sat* 10.00–20.00
Sun 11.00–18.00
Bank Holidays 11.00–18.00

Tube: Leicester Square

---

123 Oxford St
London W1R 1TF
Tel: 020 7287 3624

Open: *Mon–Fri* 08.30–19.00
(*Thu* till 20.00)
Sat 10.00–19.00
Sun 12.00–18.00

Tube: Oxford Circus,
Tottenham Court Road

Great for flapjacks, dried fruit, nuts, vegan chocolate, drinks and snacks like pastries and pies.

Lush Carnaby

Cruelty-free cosmetics

40 Carnaby Street, London W1V
Tel: 020–7287 5874

Open: *Mon–Wed* 10.00–19.00
Thu–Sat 10.00–20.00
Sun 12.00–18.00

Tube: Oxford Circus

Lovely cosmetics, 70% vegan.

Berwick Street Market

Fruit and veg market

Pedestrianised south end of
Berwick Street, W1

Open: *Mon–Sat* 09.00–18.00

Fruit and veg market with bargains in £1 bowls. Also a flower stall and a dried fruit and nuts stall.

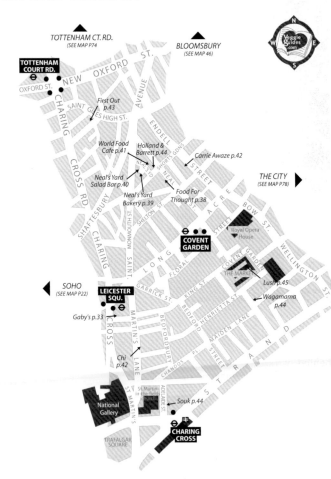

COVENT GARDEN
Central London

TOTTENHAM CT. RD.
(SEE MAP P74)

BLOOMSBURY
(SEE MAP 46)

VeggieGuides.com

TOTTENHAM COURT RD.

OXFORD ST.

NEW OXFORD ST.

SAINT GILES HIGH ST.

First Out p.43

CHARING CROSS RD.

SHAFTESBURY

MONMOUTH ST.

SHELTON ST.

SAINT MARTIN'S

ENDELL ST.

SHORTS GDNS

NEAL ST.

NEAL'S YARD

World Food Cafe p.41

Holland & Barrett p.44

Carrie Awaze p.42

Neal's Yard Salad Bar p.40

Neal's Yard Bakery p.39

Food For Thought p.38

COVENT GARDEN

Royal Opera House

BOW ST.

WELLINGTON ST.

COVENT GARDEN THE MARKET

Lush p.45

Wagamama p.44

THE CITY
(SEE MAP P78)

LONG ACRE

FLORAL ST.

KING ST.

SOHO
(SEE MAP P22)

LEICESTER SQ.

GARRICK ST.

BEDFORD ST.

HENRIETTA ST.

MAIDEN LANE

STRAND

Gaby's p.33

Chi p.42

CHANDOS PL.

ADELAIDE ST.

ST. MARTIN'S LANE

BEDFORDBURY

St Martin-in-the-fields church

Souk p.44

National Gallery

TRAFALGAR SQUARE

CHARING CROSS

Neal's Yard

Covent Garden has two focuses from a veggie's point of view: Neal's Yard in the north and the Piazza in the south, linked by Neal Street.

The area around Neal's Yard, Long Acre and Neal Street is jam packed with unique and amazing shops and all sorts of designer gear. Stock up at a very large Holland & Barrett, behind which is Neal's Yard itself, a courtyard with three superb daytime vegetarian cafes, an apothecary, a store that makes custom rubber stamps, and Neal's Yard Meeting Rooms where you can find green events, personal development and alternative therapy courses. If you want to stuff yourself at lunchtime try the World Food Café, or have a drink and light meal at Neal's Yard Salad Bar or Neal's Yard Bakery (closing for expansion and renovation until January 2005). If you're after a fast lunch, pop around the corner to the basement Food for Thought, one of London's oldest vegetarian restaurants.

At the south end of Neal Street, continue down James Street past the tube station to Covent Garden 'proper' with its street theatre in the Piazza, the covered crafts market, and the complex of trendy shops including a branch of Lush, the gorgeous smelling soaps and bodycare store that has hundreds of animal free delights and all clearly labelled in their free catalogue.

World Food Cafe

Food for Thought

*Vegan &
veggie restaurant*

Open:

Mon–Sat 12.00–20.30
Sun   12.00–17.00
No credit cards. Non Smoking
They do catering.
Unlicensed, BYO, free corkage.

31 Neal Street, Covent Garden
London, WC2H 9PR
Tel: 020–7836 9072 (office)
                     /0239 (restaurant)
Tube: Covent Garden

See map on page 36

Extremely popular veggie take-away and café on fascinating Neal Street in a vaulted basement. Pine tables and buzzy, cosmopolitan atmosphere. They offer good value and a global menu. Crowded at peak times and you'll need to queue on the stairs at lunchtime for counter service. Many dishes are vegan or vegan option.

Menu changes daily, here are some examples: vegan carrot and butterbean soup or butternut squash soup £2.90; two bean salad, pasta with pesto, potato salad with tofu mayo, all £3 to £5

Vegan main courses £4 to £6 include Ethiopian Wat; Middle Eastern mezze; Carri coco curry; Malay sambal; shepherdess pie; satay and tofu noodles; roast Mediterranean veg with polenta; mushroom stroganoff; cauliflower & peanut arial; sir-fry veg.

The evening menu from 5pm

is slightly different with many different ingredients on a big plate, for example cannelloni filled with aubergine, sundried tomatoes and basil served with polenta, broccoli and tomato frissée salad for £6.00 to £6.50.

Scrummy vegan desserts such as strawberry and vanilla scones, apple and plum crumble or fruit salad £1.20 to £3.00. Lots of drinks including fresh juices, tea, coffee, soya milk.

If you like this you'll probably like the cafes round the corner in Neal's Yard too, though to be honest there is nowhere quite like this place.

Neal's Yard Bakery

Vegan & veggie restaurant

Open:

Mon–Sat 10.30–17.00
Sun closed

Reopening early 2005.
Kids welcome

6 Neal's Yard, Covent Garden,
London WC2H 9DP
Tel: 020-7836 5199
Tube: Covent Garden

See map on page 36

Café with patio, seating downstairs and up overlooking the courtyard. They are closed till around end January 2005 for renovation, relocating the ground floor bakery elsewhere to make more space for seating, planning to open earlier for organic breakfasts and summer evenings.

Soups, salads, hot dishes and desserts to eat in or take away, plus all kinds of bread. The menu changes regularly and there is always a vegan option.

Some typical soups have been roasted red pepper and garlic, or split pea and mint for £2.70 small portion or £2.95 regular, add 35p for eat-in. There are four salads daily and they are all vegan, small or regular portions £3.00 to £3.35, slightly more for eat-in.

For mains you could try the sweet potato and spinach and korma or mushroom and

cashew biriyani, both vegan for £3.50 small or £3.90 regular. Wide range of organic pastries, many vegan and/or wheat-free.

They have several dessert items of which some are vegan like the fruit and nut bars or coconut cookies, plus cakes, which can be sugar free, organic and/or vegan for £1.25.

License pending.

If you like this you'll probably like the other cafes in Neal's Yard or Food For Thought round the corner.

Neal's Yard Salad Bar

International vegetarian café and restaurant

Open: *Every day* 08.30–21.00
till 22.00/22.30 in summer
Smoking area in separate room.
Children welcome, high chairs.
Lots of food kids love like pizza,
spaghetti, shakes, cakes.
Licensed. Birthday cakes. Parties.

2, 8–10 Neal's Yard,
Covent Garden, WC2H 9DP
Tel: 020-7836 3233
Tube: Covent Garden,
Tottenham Ct. Rd.
www.nealsyardsaladbar.co.uk
See map on page 36

Brazilian vegan owned vegetarian wholefood café downstairs with tables inside and out, and a restaurant upstairs. Vegan, wheat and yeast free clearly marked.

Six breakfasts 08.30–12.00 £2.75, £3.85, £6.05 from toast and peanut butter to full English with everything.

Mon–Fri take–away large special £4.

Soup £5.50 (£2.50–3.00 take-way). Appetizers such as olives, stuffed aubergine, Snacks like sundried tomato rice bread, vegan quiche, pumpkin polenta pie, bruschetta £1.90–6.50. 5 salads £5.50–£6.50.

Daily specials £8.25–9.50. Specialities £10.50 such as Brazilian feijoada of black beans, soya meat, rice, finger tapioca, fried banana, farofa and pumpkin; spaghetti bolognese with minced soya meat. Vegan hamburger with finger tapioca and side salad £7.15. Vegan soyannaise pizza £5.50.

9 desserts, 5 vegan, £3.85 such as berries and ginger tart with almond, apple pie, mango trifle, banana and cinamon cake. Muffins £1.90.

Juices and shakes include exotic Brazilian fruits. Hot drinks include soyaccino £2.20. 500ml beer £3.85. Sangria £3.85, jug £15.50. House wine £3.85, bottle £15.50.

World Food Cafe

International veggie restaurant

Open:

Mon–Fri 11.30–16.30
Sat 11.30–17.00
Sun closed

Kids welcome
Visa, MC over £10
Non smoking

First Floor, 14 Neal's Yard
Covent Garden,
London WC2H 9DP

Tel: 020-7379-0298

Tube: Covent Garden,
Tottenham Ct. Rd.

See map on page 36

Upstairs international wholefood vegetarian restaurant, overlooking Neal's Yard. 90% vegan. There's an open plan kitchen in the centre so you can see all the food being prepared. A sign of a good vegetarian restaurant is that 75% of the customers are not vegetarian, they just like the environment and the food.

Desserts £3.45, vegan flapjack £1.50.

Fresh fruit juice £2.25, fresh lime soda £1.95, herb teas (pot) or barleycup £1.50, cafetiere £1.55. They have soya milk.

Minimum charge £5.00 at lunchtime and all day Saturday.

Meals from every continent £6.85 such as Indian spicy veg masala with steamed brown rice; falafel. Small mixed salad £4.85. Soup of the day £3.85.

Big meals £7.95 could be thali; Turkish meze; West African sweet potatoes and cabbage in creamy groundnut and cayenne sauce served with fresh banana, steamed brown rice and salad; Mexican platter; large mixed plate of all the day's salads.

If you like this you'll probably like the new international vegan restaurant 222 in West London, The Gate (Hammersmith) or Manna (Camden & Primrose Hill, North London).

Carrie Awaze

Omnivorous sandwich shop

27 Endell Street
Covent Garden, London WC2

Tel: 020-7836 0815

Open: Mon-Fri 10.30-20.00
Sat 12.00-18.00
Sun 10.30-20.00

Tube: Covent Garden

Omnivorous Indian and international take-away with stacks for veggies and vegans for 15 years.

Soup £2.95 or take out £1.95.

6 vegan and 21 veggie sandwiches £2.50-3.25 take-away, £2.50-3.80 eat in, such as "Brown Bomber" onion bhajia with hummous and salad.

Filled jacket spud £5.95-6.25 such as "Arne Street" with dhal and onion bhajia, or with veg curry and cashews. Main meal £7.95 such as vegetarian or vegan thali, curry and rice, or Hyderabadi korma with veg and fruit.

Fresh fruit salad is the only vegan dessert.

Beer £2.25 with food. Wine £9.95 bottle or £2.95 mini bottle. Herb or green tea, (decaf) tea £1.25, (decaf) coffee £1.50, cappuccino £1.75, Indian chai, they have soya milk.

Heartbeat award from Camden. No smoking. No mobiles inside unless you're a doctor or nurse.

Chi

Chinese vegan buffet restaurant

55 St Martin's Lane
Covent Garden, London WC2

Tel: 020-7836 3434

Open: Every day: 12.00-23.00
Sun 12.00-22.00

Tube: Leicester Square,
Charing Cross

All you can eat Chinese vegan buffet restaurant, like the busier one in Greek Street (Soho), one block back from Charing Cross Road in the heart of theatreland.

Fill up at the West End's best value restaurant on fried and boiled rice, noodles, stir-fry vegetables, tofu, mushrooms and several kinds of fake meat, with as many visits to the buffet as you like for just £5 before 5.30pm, then £6 afterwards and all day Sunday.

Take-away £3 or £4 for a large box. No credit cards

First Out

Gay & lesbian vegetarian cafe

52 St Giles High St
London WC2H 8LH
Tel: 020-7240 8042
Open: *Mon-Sat* 10.00-23.00
Sun 11.00-22.30
Tube: Tottenham Court Rd

Smart, modern and very popular gay and lesbian vegetarian café with international menu and basement bar. Music for all tastes and low enough not to be intrusive. Can be lively or very laid back depending on time of day.

The soup of the day is always vegan for £3.50. Range of platters such as mezze with dips and pitta bread for £4.50. On Sundays they do brunch.

For main course you could try the veg chilli or veg curry, pies, bakes, or nachos from £4.95-5.45.

Generally good for vegans until you get to the many cakes, but they do have some home made vegan flapjacks. Soya milk on request.

Glass of house white £2.95-£3.95, £12-16 a bottle. Beer £2.50-2.85. Smoking only in the bar downstairs.

They have party evenings and Friday night is 'Girl Friday' or women's night with men as guests. Visa, MC.

The Cafe, LSE

Omnivorous café

East Buildings Basement
Houghton Street, Aldwych
London WC2 2AE
Tel: 020-7955-7164
Open: *Mon-Fri*
9.00-18.00 term
10.00-16.00 holidays
Tube: Temple

Student basement café in the London School of Economics, no longer completely veggie but with lots of options for veggies, some vegan. These may change daily and prices are very reasonable.

Several veggie kosher sandwiches, including avocado with mixed leaf or roasted veg, and filled bagels £1-£2 such as veg fake chicken, houmous and salad. Italian panini with roasted five-bean hummous.

The soup of the day is always vegetarian or vegan, such as tomato and basil with mixed veg, or minestrone, £1 a cup or £1.30 with a roll.

Salads £1.10– £2.30 might include pasta with tomato, or couscous salad with mixed veg.

Fair Trade coffee 60p small, 70p large, espresso, cappuccino, but no soya milk.

Please note that opening hours vary according to term times.

Wagamama Covent Gdn

Japanese Omnivorous

1a Tavistock Street
Covent Garden
London WC2E 7PE
Tel: 020-7836 3330
Open: *Mon–Sat* 12.00-23.00
      Sun   12.30-22.00
Tube: Covent Garden

Omnivorous fast food Japanese noodle bar with some extremely filling veggie and vegan dishes.

See Bloomsbury branch for menu. (page 51)

The Souk

Arabian omnivorous restaurant

8 Adelaide Street
London WC2N 4HZ
(opposite Charing Cross Station next to St Martins Church market)

Tel: 020-7240 2337
Open: *Mon–Fri* 08.00-19.00
      Thu   till 20.00
      Sat–Sun closed
Tube: Charing Cross

This Moroccan / Med take-away/snack bar serves really good vegan wraps such as houmus, falafel and salad, bean and salad wraps, hot spicy sweet potato wraps, stuffed vine leaves, plus one vegan salad – all ready wrapped or sold in little containers to take away. The sweets are fresh fruit salad, and baklava. They also sell fruit smoothies and other drinks to take away or eat in.

Holland & Barrett

Healthfood shop

21 Shorts Gardens
Covent Garden, London WC2H
Tel: 020-7379 0298
Open: *Mon–Sat* 10.00-19.00
      Sun   11-17.30
Tube: Covent Garden,
      Tottenham Court Rd

Big health food shop by the entrance to Neal's Yard with its three veggie cafes. Some take-away food such as pasties and rolls. (For fresh organic fruit and veg go to the nearby Tesco Metro.) Every 4-6 weeks a qualified nutritionist offers food sensitivity testing for £39, combined with vitamin and mineral deficiency testing £45, E-numbers £16 more.

Holland & Barrett

Healthfood shop

Unit 16,
Embankment Shopping Centre,
Villiers St, London WC2 6NN

Tel: 020-7839 4988

Open: *Mon-Fri* 08.00-19.00
     Sat   09-18.00
     Sun   11-18.00

Tube: Embankment
      Charing Cross

Down the left side of Charing Cross station. Lots of veggie snacks and take-aways including pies, pastries and cakes.

Lush Covent Garden

Cruelty-free cosmetics

11 The Piazza, Covent Garden,
London WC2E 8RB

Tel: 020-7240 4570

Tube: Covent Garden

Cruelty-free cosmetics, 70% of them vegan and clearly labelled in their gorgeous free catalogue.

BLOOMSBURY
Central London

This mainly residential area, to the east of Tottenham Court Road and north of Covent Garden, has many midrange and budget hotels, YMCA, YWCA. There are also University College London and the giant Generator backpacker hostel, hence the streets are thronged with young people from all over the world. The area's top attraction is the British Museum, the largest of London's 150 museums, featuring Egyptian mummies, Greek and Roman antiquities and other British Empire loot.

Our favourite road is Marchmont Street with cafes, take-aways, a cinema nearby and a real community feel. Indian restaurant Vegetarian Paradise has a lunchtime bargain buffet and Alara whole-foods store opposite has a veggie café, take-aways and extremely charming staff.

Fancy a day off lounging on the grass reading a novel? In summer load up with picnic munchies at Alara or Planet Organic (see Tottenham Court Road) and head for tranquil Russell Square, Bloomsbury Square, Gordon Square (week days only, full of students revising) or Queen Square. For more typically British weather, next to Queen Square you'll find a vegetarian café without crowds in the basement of Mary Ward adult education centre.

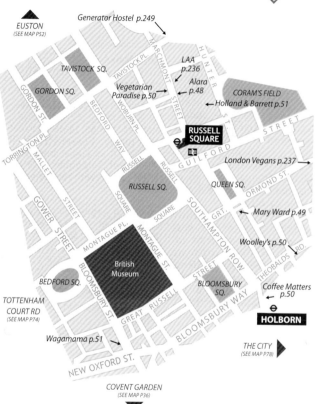

EUSTON
(SEE MAP P52)

Generator Hostel p.249

TAVISTOCK SQ.

GORDON SQ.

GORDON ST.

TORRINGTON PL.

MALLET   STREET

GOWER   STREET

BEDFORD   WAY

WOBURN PL.

TAVISTOCK PL.

MARCHMONT   STREET

HUNTER   STREET

LAA
p.236

Vegetarian
Paradise p.50

Alara
p.48

CORAM'S FIELD

← Holland & Barrett p.51

RUSSELL
SQUARE

RUSSELL

RUSSELL

GUILFORD   STREET

London Vegans p.237 →

RUSSELL SQ.

SQUARE

MONTAGUE PL.

MONTAGUE ST.

QUEEN SQ.

SOUTHAMPTON   ROW

GRT.

ORMOND ST.

GRT.

← Mary Ward p.49

Woolley's p.50

THEOBALDS   RD.

British
Museum

BEDFORD SQ.

BLOOMSBURY ST.

BLOOMSBURY
SQ.

Coffee Matters
← p.50

HOLBORN

TOTTENHAM
COURT RD
(SEE MAP P74)

GREAT   RUSSELL   STREET

BLOOMSBURY WAY

THE CITY
(SEE MAP P78)

Wagamama p.51

NEW OXFORD ST.

COVENT GARDEN
(SEE MAP P36)

47

Alara

Open:

Mon–Fri 9.00–18.00
Sat   10–18.00
Sun   closed

MC, Visa
5% discount to members of local
Fitness First gym.

58 Marchmont Street
Bloomsbury, London WC1N 1AB
Tel: 020–7837 1172
Tube: Russell Square

See map on page 47

Family run vegetarian healthfood shop in a lovely street that is very popular with locals, facing Vegetarian Paradise Indian restaurant and next to the Marchmont Community Centre where London Animal Action meets on the second Monday evening of the month. There are 6 cafe tables each seating 4 people and a large take-away section – one of the best places to grab lunch to go. Popular with local residents and office workers, students from the nearby universities, tourists and backpackers from the many hotels and the Generator hostel around the corner.

Help yourself to 100% organic salads and hot food, 85p per 100g, such as chickpea salad and gluten-free veg curries. Microwave on premises. Organic, gluten-free and sugar-free cakes.

Hot drinks are all organic such as herbal teas 80p, moccaccino £1.59.

Freshly made organic juices £1.89 small, £2.69 large, such as orange, apple, carrot with ginger. Cockails £2.39–2.79 such as apple, beetroot and carrot. Smoothies £2.99–3.99, can be with rice or soya milk.

Stacks of vegan and organic produce in several aisles, including fruit & veg, wide variety of bread, own brand muesli, Swedish Glace vegan ice-cream, frozen foods. Organic juices and fruit smoothies, selection of veggie beers, and wines at Christmas. Supplements, cosmetics, essential oils.

They have experienced and charming staff to give advice about nutrition. Food allergy testing by appointment.

If you like this you'll probably like Bumblebee, another fabulous wholefood store in Brecknock Road, north London.

Mary Ward

Vegetarian Café

Open:	Term time
Mon–Thu	9.30–21.00
Fri	9.30–20.30
Sat	9.30–16.00

Sun: once per month when the centre is open 11–15.00

Kids welcome, small portions
Cheques but no credit cards.
Non Smoking

42 Queen Square
Bloomsbury
London WC1N 3AQ
Tel: 020-7831 7711
Tube: Russell Sq, Holborn

See map on page 47

Completely vegetarian cafe in an adult education centre by green Queens Square. Modern and bright with monthly changing art exhibits. Friendly Italian owners so expect a Mediterranean flavour on the menu which changes daily.

Breakfast served until 11.45, usually toasties, jam and Danish pastries.

The lunch menu includes daily changing salads with four choices which include vegan and wheat-free, £1.95 small, £2.95 large.

They bake bread on the premises such as herby garlic bread, spinach and cumin.

Light meals £3 include stuffed baguettes, such as red lentil and olive pate with lettuce; soup (always vegan), tortilla with salad; stuffed tortilla, stir-fry rice with veg; roast veg with couscous; pasta bake; potato pie; roast onion stuffed with couscous and veg. £3.50 with mixed green salad or £4.10 with a big salad.

Cakes 80–95p, none vegan but they are working on it.

Plenty of cold drinks such as Purdeys and Aqua Libra, fresh juices, coffees and herbal teas, soyacinno, soya chocolate and barleycup. Not licensed.

Near London Vegans' last Wed!nesday venue (see Local Groups) so a great place to unwind beforehand.

If you like this you'll probably like spending an afternoon at Pogo Cafe or the Gallery Cafe in East London.

Vegetarian Paradise

Indian restaurant & take-away

59 Marchmont Street
Bloomsbury
London WC1N 1AP
Tel: 020-7278 6881

Open: *Mon–Sun* 12-15.00
17.00-24.00

Tube: Russell Square

Indian vegetarian restaurant offering real value for money with a lunch time buffet, all you can eat for £4.50 per adult.

Hot starters, £2.10-£2.50, include ragara pattice, stuffed potato cakes with spicy chick peas. Cold starters like pani poori – hollow wholewheat pooris served with tamarind and dates, spicy sauces and boiled chick peas for £2.45.

Mains from £3.50 for curries or £3.95 for a plain dosa; thalis from £4.95. Desserts from £1.95.

Bring your own alcohol, no corkage charge. Soft drinks £1.10.

Separate smoke-free area and party room available for up to 40 people.

Woolley's

Vegetarian take-away

33 Theobalds Road
London WC1X 8XP
Tel: 020-7405 3028

Open: *Mon–Fri* 07.30-15.3
Sat–Sun closed

Tube: Holborn & Chancery Lane

Take-away food. 10 salads with raw and cooked vegan options such as organic wild rice with peanuts, parsley and red peppers in sweet pickle dressing. Vegan pies and pasties, baked potatoes, soups occasionally vegan and some cakes (not vegan). Fresh every day and able to cater for gluten free. Innocent juices, dirnks, bottled water, tea, coffee but no soya milk. Fax your order through on 020-7430-2417. They also do catering and wholesale sandwiches.

Coffee Matters

Organic coffee bar

4 Southampton Row
nr Holborn Tube, Holborn,
London WC1
Tel: 020-7242 9090

Open: *Mon–Sat* 7.00-18.00
Sat 9.00-15.00
Sun closed

Tube: Holborn

Organic coffee bar serving Fairtrade coffee, tea, hot chocolate, organic sandwiches, snacks, and cakes. Organic canned drinks. Organic soya milk. Vegan sandwiches include alfalfa sprout with tomato, and hummous on tomato bread. Also falafel and salad. No smoking.

Wagamama

Omnivorous Japanese restaurant

4A Streatham Street
off Bloomsbury St.
London WC1A 1JB
Tel: 020-7323 9223
Open: *Mon-Sat* 12-23.00
(last order)
Sun 12.30-22.00
Tube: Tottenham Court Rd

This was the first of many Japanese noodle bars listed in this book, with over nine veggie and vegan dishes, long trestle tables and very noisy. Not great for a first date, but superb if you're out on the town for a laff. When each dish is cooked it is served straiight away, so a group may get their food at different times.

Raw mixed juices £2.70.

Mains include veg soup with wholemeal ramen noodles,

stir-fried veg and tofu £6.65; yasai katsu curry with rice, mixed leaves and pickles £6.35. Also two sauce based noodle dishes.

Side dishes £1.30-£5.70 like five grilled veg dumpling; miso soup; skewers of chargrilled veg coated in yakitori sauce; and freshly steamed green soya beans.

6 desserts, £3.50-£4.25, of which fresh papaya is vegan.

Wine from £11 a bottle, £3.15 a glass; beers from £2.90; sake from £2.95.

Menus at
www.wagamama.com

Holland & Barrett

Healthfood store

36 Brunswick Shopping Ctr
London WC1N 1AE
Tel: 020-7278 4640
Open: *Mon-Sat* 9.30-17.30
Sun closed
Tube: Russell Square

Small branch with many veggie/vegan munchies like dried fruit, nuts and seeds, but no fresh take-away.

EUSTON Central London

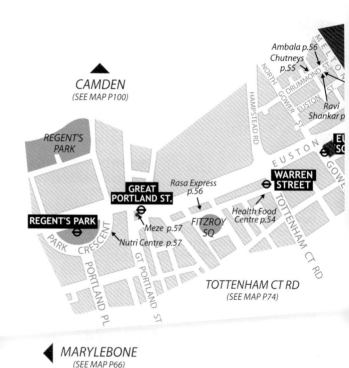

▲ CAMDEN
(SEE MAP P100)

Ambala p.56
Chutneys
p.55

Ravi
Shankar p.

REGENT'S
PARK

NORTH GOWER ST.

DRUMMOND ST.

EUSTON ST.

HAMPSTEAD RD

EUSTON

EU
SQ

WARREN
STREET

GREAT
PORTLAND ST.

Rasa Express
p.56

REGENT'S PARK

Health Food
Centre p.54

FITZROY
SQ

Meze p.57

Nutri Centre p.57

PARK CRESCENT

GT PORTLAND ST.

TOTTENHAM CT RD

PORTLAND PL.

TOTTENHAM CT RD
(SEE MAP P74)

GOWE

◀ MARYLEBONE
(SEE MAP P66)
▼

ISLINGTON
(SEE MAP P112)

EUSTON
🚆 ⊖
· Diwana p.55

ROAD

.56

JSTON
QUARE

BLOOMSBURY
(SEE MAP P46)

Euston Station is the gateway to most places north or north-west of London, so you'll likely end up there sometime. As train food is so awful for vegetarians and vegans, why not tank up on grub before or after your journey at any of half a dozen great eateries.

Drummond Street has three great value vegetarian Indian restaurants, the perfect place to end your day even if you're not going out of town. There's also an Indian sweet shop with samosas and other snacks.

Health Food Centre, down the side of Warren Street tube station, has the most amazing selection of vegetarian sandwiches in London and lots of hot take-away food. And there's a fruit stall opposite.

New in this edition are Meze cafe at the top of Great Portland Street, open long hours and handy for Regent's Park, and Rasa Express with a few snacks for a quick weekday lunch.

Health Food Centre

Health food shop and takeaway

Open:

Mon–Fri	08.30–18.30
Sat	12.00–16.00
Sun	closed

Visa, MC, Amex

11 Warren Street
Euston, London NW1

Tel: 020 7387 9289

Tube: Warren Street,
Euston, Euston Square

See map on page 53

Vegetarian health food shop and take-away tucked away down the side of Warren Street tube. The owner Raj is very friendly and a committed veggie and has added a juice and coffee bar with a table outside, weather permitting. Handy for Euston or Regent's Park.

London's biggest range of veggie and vegan sandwiches, such as (fake) chicken and salad; lentil burger and houmous with salad; date, walnut and banana; veggie burger and houmous; veggie BLT. Plus filled topedos, baps and baguettes. All £3 for two which is stunning value for central London.

Savouries like spicy Mexican slice, cartons of pasta and couscous salad.

Very popular hot take-away dishes include organic brown rice with vegan curries, and pasta bake, £4, or £2.50 for a small one.

Lots of cakes, some sugar free or suitable for vegans like date crumble.

The juice bar has combos like apple, ginger and orange for £1.30 medium, £1.99 large. Energy drinks like spirulina, echinacea or guarana around £2.50. Vegan fruit smoothie £1.40.

Coffee, teas, soyaccino £1.30 for a largish cup.

The shop packs a lot of wholefoods into a small space. Extensive range of cruelty-free toiletries, herbal remedies and oils.

Vitamins, minerals and some wholefoods.

10% discount if you mention this book.

If you like the sandwiches here you'll be pleased to find they're also available at the Union Street Newsagent, see South Bank. (Central London)

Chutneys

Vegetarian South Indian

124 Drummond Street
Euston, London NW1 2HL

Tel: 020-7388-0604

Open: *Mon-Sat* 12.00-14.45
dinner 18-22.30
(last orders), close 23.00
Sun 12-22.00 (last
order)
Lunch buffet

Tube: Euston, Euston Square

Vegetarian South Indian restaurant. Wide variety of dishes and special Keralan feast menu available most days. A popular place for a quiet romantic dinner that won't stretch the wallet.

Eat as much as you like buffet from 12 noon to 2.45pm every day for £5.95, Sunday all day.

There are 16 starters such as bhel poori, £2.20 to £3.00.

Main courses include nine kinds of dosa £2.80-4.85, 11 curries £2.50-3.40. Plenty of whole wheat breads, pickles; salad and rice from 90p.

Thalis start at £3.95. If you are really hungry try the excellent Chutney's deluxe thali for £7.95 with dhal soup, 4 curries, pillau rice, chutneys, chappatis or pooris and dessert.

Five desserts £1.60-£1.80 but we couldn't see anything for vegans.

Diwana

Vegetarian South Indian

121-123 Drummond Street
Euston, London NW1 2HL
Tel: 020-7387 5556

Open: *Mon-Sat* 12.00-23.30
Sun 12.00-22.30

Tube: Euston, Euston Square,
Warren St

One of the larger vegetarian Indian restaurants on Drummond Street, established over twenty five years. Light wood décor and lots of potted palms give a relaxed and informal feel. The food is inexpensive and tasty. They offer an eat as much as you like lunch buffet 12-14.30 every day for £6.50 which has different dishes daily, and also a full a la carte menu all day.

Lots of starters such as dahi vada chick peas £3.00, masala spring rolls £3.50.

Thalis £5.50-7.75.

Lots of dosas £5.50-5.95 and vegetable side dishes

like bombay aloo and aloo gobi £3.80–4.20.

Several desserts, alas as in most Indian restaurants there is nothing for vegans.

Diwana are not licensed but you can bring your own with no corkage charge. There is an off licence next door.

Ravi Shankar

Vegetarian South Indian restaurant

133–135 Drummond Street
Euston, London NW1 2HL

Tel: 020–7388 6458

Open: *Mon–Sat* 12.00–22.45
(last orders 22.00)

Tube: Euston, Euston Square

One of three great value vegetarian South Indian restaurants in this street next to Euston station. Daily specials throughout the week. There's always plenty for vegans.

Set 3 course meal £7.85, two courses £6.55, or have a dosa or curry £5.15–5.60.

On a Monday they serve cauliflower potato curry for £4.50, Tuesday is veg biriyani with curry for £4.25, and each day the specials are different. Sat £4.75, Sun £4.55.

Desserts, but none vegan.

Wine £7.95 bottle, £1.80 glass. Most cards accepted.

Ambala

Vegetarian take-away

112/114 Drummond Street
Euston, London NW1 2HN

Tel: 020 7387 7886 / 3521

Open: *Mon–Sat* 8.30–18.30
Sun 9.00–18.30

Tube: Euston

Vegetarian take-away and sweet shop opposite Ravi Shankar and Diwana, for when you need to eat on the run. Samosas and pakoras but not much for vegans.

Rasa Express

Vegetarian and fish fast food

327 Euston Road,
London NW1 3AD

Tel: 020-7387 8974

Open: *Mon–Fri* 12-15.00
Sat–Sun closed

Tube: Great Portland St

Indian Keralan vegetarian and fish fast food restaurant with a bright pink front just west of Tottenham Court Road. Small menu but amazing value for central London. Starters £1.50

include potato cakes with ginger and curry leaves; veg samosas. Masala dosa £2.75. Lunch box £2.95 for rice, bread, a stir-fried vegetable, two curries and sweet of the day. Bananas and mangoes. Cash only.

NB: The CTJ nearby on Euston Road has closed as we go to press. So if you want Chinese, try the two branches nearby listed in the Tottenham Court Rd section.

Meze Cafe

Turkish omnivorous cafe

305 Great Portland Street, London W1W 5DA

Open: *Every day 08-23.00*
Tube: Great Portland Street

Handy for Regent's Park, this is a big all-day Turkish omnivorous café next to Great Portland Street underground station and opposite International House student hostel. Tables inside and out. Open for breakfast, lunch and dinner, and chilling out at any time. Meze and salad buffet £3.90 eat in (£3 take out), large £4.90 (£3.90), including pitta bread. Choose from Turkish wraps; most of the cold (£3) and several hot (£4) meze are

veggie or vegan. There are two grocers, a Pret-a-Manger and two pubs opposite.

Nutri Centre

Cruelty free cosmetics & food

7 Park Crescent,
London W1N

Tel: 020-7436-5122

Open: *Mon-Sat* 9.00-19.00
Sat 10-19.00
Sun closed

Tube: Regents Park,
Great Portland St

In the basement of a natural health centre, this shop sells mainly supplements and body care products, plus a few foods like pasta

There is a big books section with a separate telephone: 020-7323 2382. They have an impressive mail order books catalogue.

www.nutricentre.com

SOUTH BANK
Central London *by Christine Klein*

Waterloo is not a part of London you associate with vegetarian or vegan food!! Close by along the River Thames are the London Eye, Festival Hall, Gabriel's Wharf (an interesting place by the river to meander if you like craft shops and bars), the IMAX cinema, the National Theatre, National Film Theatre, the Young Vic and Old Vic Theatres, and of course Waterloo Station itself – gateway to the continent. But where can a hungry veggie eat?

Tucked away behind Waterloo Station lies a street called Lower Marsh, where there is a bustling street market. There has been a market here since the mid 19th century and this road is now a conservation area, in recognition of its special character, and also that the earliest records (1377) of this area show that it was the sight of the ancient Lambeth Marsh. Here you can buy cheap vegetables and fruit of a high quality, plus inexpensive clothes, shoes and cd's. Here and there are a few unusual shops selling trendy and ethnic jewellery, antiques, cards, not forgetting the fetish shop, with its black plastic ensembles, and art gallery – truly something for everyone!! Lower Marsh also has a few street food stalls as well, which all offer veggie options. Crossing Waterloo Road, Lower Marsh becomes the Cut, which also has numerous cafes and bars where a hungry herbivore can eke out a few meals.

Although Waterloo has only one truly veggie eating place, Coopers – sadly not open in the evening, don't despair, tasty veggie and vegan food can be found elsewhere in the vicinity and for a reasonable price. The place has been changing and there are numerous trendy bars and cafes springing up all over, as well as some lovely cosy back street pubs such as the Kings Arms in the Cornwell Road/ Rupell Street area.

Coopers

Vegetarian cafe and deli

17 Lower Marsh
London SE1

Open:

Mon–Fri 08.30–17.30
Sat–Sun closed

17 Lower Marsh
London SE1

Tel: 020–7261 9314

Tube: Waterloo
See map on page 59

Long established and very popular vegetarian family run cafe, deli and health food store. All dishes are cooked fresh on the day on the premises. Good value for both veggies and vegans, with excellent and imaginative vegan rolls and sandwiches to take away or eat in. Better than other sandwich bars for quality and size of fillings. A good spot to have lunch or afternoon tea.

They serve a variety of vegan savouries like potato and onion bhaji, veg and sunflower rissole, carrot and onion cutlet, chickpea roti, various kebabs and cottage pies.

Appetizers too, for example olives, vine leaves and houmous.

They always have a selection of salads with a minimum of one vegan. Soup is often vegan too.

Several types of sandwich like veg sausage and pickle, Swiss herb paté and houmous, peanut butter, all with salad.

Normally a choice of 5 cakes daily like chocolate and walnut, carrot and coconut, apple and sultana, at least one is vegan.

Hot chocolate and coffee (soya milk available) and herb teas.

Wonderful health food store with lots of the latest products and lovely breads and deli type food. Organic beers and ciders.

Staff are very helpful and will always order things for you if they don't have it in stock.

If you like this you'll probably like the cafes inside the Planet Organic stores in Fulham (West London) and off Tottenham Court Road (Central).

Tas

Turkish/Anatolian omnivorous restaurant

Open:

Mon–Fri 12.00–23.30
Sun 12.00–22.30
Children welcome, one high chair.
MC, Visa, Amex. Smoking area.
12.5% service charge.

33 The Cut, Waterloo,
London SE1 8LF
Tel: 020-7928 1444
Tube: Waterloo
www.tasrestaurant.com
See map on page 59

Turkish omnivorous. Anatolian restaurant that received the Time Out Best Vegetarian Meal Award 2000. Almost all starters (meze) are veggie. The menu has a veggie section with 10 main dishes.

Cold starters £3.55 to £4.25 include kisir: crushed walnuts, hazelnuts, bulgar wheat, tomato sauce, herbs, fresh mint, and spring onions; zetin yagli patlican: aubergine, tomatoes, garlic, peppers and chickpeas cooked in olive oil; and the classic Turkish dolma: stuffed vine leaves with pine kernels.

Also several veggie hot starters like sebzeli kofte, which is falafel with broad beans.

Vegetarian main dishes £6.55–7.45 such as patli–canli: grilled aubergine with tomatoes, peppers and couscous; spinach with potaotes; okra with herbs;

baklali enginar: artichokes, broad beans, fresh tomatoes with garlic; vegetarian couscous. Four veggie salads and the usual rice dishes like bademli pilaf with almonds and kayisili pilaf with apricot for £1.45 to £2.95.

Many desserts £3.35–3.55 though according to their online menu only the fruit salad is vegan.

Wines £11.95–19.50 bottle.

Live guitar music in the evenings. Parties and special occasions welcome.

There is another branch between Borough and London Bridge tube stations at 72 Borough High Street, SE1 1XF. Tel: 020 7403 7200/7277. And a similar Tas Pide restaurant near the Tate Modern at 20-22 New Globe Walk, SE1 9DR. Tel: 020 7928 3300 / 7633 9777.

If you like this you'll probably like Tas Firin in Bethnal Green Road (East London) or The Dervish in Stoke Newington (North London).

Meson Don Felipe

Omnivorous Spanish bar

53A The Cut , SE1 8LF
Tel: 020-7928 3237

Open: *Mon–Sat* 12.00–24.00
Sun closed

Tube: Waterloo

Omnivorous Spanish bar with 10 vegetarian tapas snacks like lentils and fresh vegetables, artichoke heart salad, chickpeas with spinach, and deep fried aubergines for £3.50–4.50. House wine from £10 to £70 a bottle.

It gets crowded prior to performances at the Old or Young Vic theatres nearby.

Paradiso

Omnivorous Italian restaurant

61 The Cut, SE1 8LL
Tel: 020 7261 1221

Open: *Every day* 12–24.00

Tube: Waterloo

Loads of the usual Italian veggie options in this smart clean Sicilian restaurant. There are a couple of vegan dishes and most of the veggie pizzas can be made with no cheese. Of the 45 dishes, half are veggie. Part of a small chain of restaurants across London which have long been a favourite of local celebrities – so we are told!

Casse-Croute

Continental style sandwich-deli bar

19 Lower Marsh, SE1 7RJ
Tel: 020 7928 4700

Open: *Mon–Fri* 06.30–16.00
Sat 08.30–15.00

Tube: Waterloo

Lovely cafe, a few yards from Coopers, to get a take-away lunch, with just a couple of seats inside. 18 different sandwiches for veggies, 6 of these vegan. Also fresh salads, cakes, and hot snacks such as veg pasta, curry etc. They are open to suggestions, so you can create your own fillings, for example avocado and salad with aubergine pate on a carrot and herb bap; humus, alfalfa, sundried tomatoes and sunflower seeds on a carrot/herb bap; roasted veg plus sundried tomato pesto on herb and tomato bread etc They do usual teas, coffees etc. Cakes are excellent – but not vegan!

Konditor & Cook

Omnivorous take-away

22 Cornwall Road, SE1 8TW
Tel: 020 7261 0456

Open: *Mon-Fri* 07.30-18.30
      Sat 08.30-14.30

Tube: Waterloo

This fantastic shop, on the corner of Roupell Street and Cornwall Rd, is very popular at lunchtime. Excellent for veggies with some vegan options, this is mostly a cake shop – but what cakes!! Everything freshly baked – lots of wonderful breads, pizzas, cakes by the the slice or whole if you're feeling greedy! At the back there is a take-away counter with soups, bakes, salads and drinks. The menu changes every day. They also serve food at The Young Vic cafe in The Cut.

Inshoku

Omnivorous Japanese restaurant

23/24 Lower Marsh, SE1 7RJ
Tel: 020 7928 2311

Open: *Mon-Fri* 12-15.00,
      18.00-23.00
      Sat 18.00-23.00
      closed Sun & bank hols.

Tube: Waterloo

Large menu with lots of vegan choices such as sweet corn cake with sweet and sour sauce, tofu with spring onions in tempura sauce for starters and veg tempura, tofu steak with veg sauce, veg ramen/ curry. They also serve the usual sushi rolls, noodle dishes and miso soup.All dishes are reasonably priced.

Cubana

Omnivorous Cuban/Creole

48 Lower Marsh, SE1 7RG
Tel: 020 7928 8778

Open: *Mon-Tue* 12-24.00
      Wed-Fri 12-01.00
      Sat 18-01.00
      Closed bank holidays
      except good Friday.

Tube: Waterloo

Another omnivourous restaurant, however, they serve a few unusual veggie options (all clearly marked on the menu) such as chickpea creole stew, sweet potato fritter with salsa, vegetable turnovers with plantain, sweet potato and veggies with salsa, and papaya salad with mango and avocado etc they also do a mixed veggie Cuban tapas for approx £7.

All cocktails are made with

freshly squeezed juices.

Service can be slow sometimes – but this is a young, lively place and gets crowded – popular with large groups.

www.cubana.co.uk

Troia

Omnivorous Turkish/Anatolian

3F Belvedere Road,
County Hall, London SE1 7GQ
Tel: 020 7633 9309

Open: *every day* 10.00 till late
Tube: Waterloo

Lots of veggie and vegan options in this new restaurant near the London Eye. A separate vegetarian set mezze for £7.75 per person, consisting of taboule, hummus, falafel, beans etc in fact 9 different dishes (a couple need substituting if you want vegan). Good mixture of both hot and cold veggie dishes on the main menu – 50% veggie of which 25% vegan.

Azzuro

Italian restaurant and wine bar

Arches 145/146, Sutton Walk,
London SE1 7ND
Tel: 020 7620 1300

Open: *Mon–Sat* 12–23.00
        Sun 12–22.30

Tube: Waterloo

Good place for large mixed groups/entertaining with a cavernous dining area under the arches of the railway line. Food is Italian with quite a few veggie options and a couple of vegan ones, such as bruschetta – tomatoes, garlic and basil on slices of bread; basil & tomato soup, various salads, lots of pizzas. Quite a good place for a lght snack and a drink pre theatre.

Wasabi Sushi

Take-away sushi bar

Villiers Street, London WC2
Tel: 020 7586 8012

Open: 11.00–23.00
Tube: Embankmemt

Off the Strand right by Embankment tube station opposite the entrance to Embankment Gardens.

They do some vegan sushi – about 10 different types at

approx £1 to £1.50 per two sushi rolls. You can pick your own pre-wrapped sushi and make up your own box of food for about £6 which is quite a lot of sushi – takeaway only.

There are avocado sushi, sweet potato and mushroom sushi, tofu with onion sushi etc. All ingredients cleary marked and they sell canned drinks plus some hot food, with one vegan dish, such as stir fried tofu noodles.

Lower Marsh Market

Street market

Lower Marsh Street
behind Waterloo Station
Open: *Mon–Fri* 9–14.00
Tube: Waterloo

Fruit and veg and just about everything for the home except furniture.

Borough Market

Huge covered food market

Between Stoney Street
and Bedale Street, SE1
Open: *Fri* 12–18.00
       Sat 9–16.00
Tube: London Bridge

This food market is the Daddy. An astounding array of stalls with exotic foods from around the the world. If you want a great foodie day out or you need something unusual like truffles to impress your dinner gusts, no other market comes close. Plenty of organic normal fruit and veg too.

Hing Loong

Chinese omnivorous restaurant

159 Borough High Street
London SE1
Tel: 020 7378 8100
Tube: Borough, London Bridge

Omnivorous Chinese restaurant recommended by vegans at the nearby PETA office. They do fab fake meat dishes like sweet and sour 'pork' and stir fried 'duck', and have an extensive veggie menu with 5 different tofu dishes. Tasty tasty.

Union Newsagents

Chinese omnivorous restaurant

77–79 Union Street
London SE1 1SG

Union News Agents (next to the League Against Cruel Sport Office) now stocks a wide selection of vegan and veggie pre-packaged sandwiches supplied by legendary sandwich shop Health Food Centre (see Euston).

65

MARYLEBONE
Central London

It's W1, but not as you know it. Unlike the party furore of Soho, this residential area between Regent's Park and Oxford Street has wide streets and ample pavement space.

Woodlands and Rasa offer classic South Indian dining, whilst newcomer Chai Pani is London's first Rajasthani Marwari Indian restaurant.

Eat & Two Veg is the other major new opening with a British and international menu plus a bar, fabulous for taking non-vegetarians to with their full English veggie breakfast, shepherd's pie and sausage and mash plus gourmet dishes from around the world.

If you need a snack whilst fashion shopping on Oxford Street, try Bean Juice café, the nearby Holland & Barrett store in the West One shopping centre at Bond Street underground, or grab a falafel from one of the Lebanese take-aways on

CAM
(SEE MAP)

REGENT'S P.

MARYLEBONE

BAKER ST.

Eat & Two V

Holland & Ba
p.72

Leaves of Life p.73

PADDINGTON

Chai Pani p.69

Wagan
p.7

MARBLE
ARCH

OXFORD

HYDE PARK

Rasa Keralan cuisine

Edgware Road.

To learn more about the health benefits of a wholefood plant based diet, and how to prepare incredibly delicious, healthy food at home, you can't do better than attend the very low cost seminars at Leaves of Life, run by medical professionals and caterers.

Woodlands Marylebone

*Vegetarian
Indian restaurant*

Open:
Every day 12–15.00,
18.00–23.00
No smoking area
MC, Visa, Amex, Diners

77 Marylebone Lane
(off Marylebone High St.)
London WIU 2PS
Tel: 020 7486 3862
Tube: Bond St, Baker St.

See map on page 67

Perhaps the largest vegetarian Indian chain in the world, with 4 London branches and 32 in India, from where the chefs come. This branch is smart with walnut flooing, cream linen and granite bar. Ideal for large parties, couples and business meetings. 75 dishes on the menu with many different flavours, textures and colours.

Starters like idli rice balls, or deep fried cashew nut pokoda, £4.25 to £4.50.

Nine varieties of dosa (vegetable stuffed pancake, made from rice and wheat) from £4.25–4.50. Their specialty is uthappam or lentil pizza, with coconut, tomato, green chilli for £5.95, extra toppings 25p. 10 curries from £4.50 to £5.95

Thalis or set meals £13.95–£15.25.

Traditional village vegetable curries and hot breads.

Many rice dishes such as pilau, lemon or coconut, £4.25. Indian breads like bathura £2.95.

7 desserts with some unusual ones like Jaggary dosa: an Indian crepe filled with pure sugar cane and cardamom at £3.95; Sheera – cream of wheat with nuts, raisins and ghee for £3.50.

Glass of house wine £2.25, bottle £10–22.50. Beer £2.75 small, £5.35 large.

They cater for parties.

www.woodlandsrestaurant.co.uk

If you like this you'll probably like their other branches in Panton Street off Leicester Square (Soho), Wembley (West London) and the newest one in Chiswick (West London).

Chai Pani

Vegetarian Rajasthani Indian restaurant and tea room

Open:
Every day 12.00–14.30
(weekends till 16.30)
18.00–22.30
Tea room 15.00–17.00
Smoking allowed but not for much longer.

64 Seymour Street,
London W1H 5BW
Tel: 020-7258 2000 / 3444
Tube: Marble Arch
MC, Visa, Amex.
Fully licensed.
See map on page 66

New Rajasthani Marwari vegetarian restaurant. The food is unique in London, prepared by sisters Jyoti and Sandhya Goenka. Big thali style plates, amazing regional costumes, candles. All you can eat thali specialists, lots of vegetables and lentils, textured breads, aromatic sweet and savoury dishes made from herbs, nuts, berries. Afternoon tea room 3–5pm offers juices and snacks like samosas, chaats and lentil pancakes plus Indian sweets.

10 thalis £6.20 including vegan, wheat-free and London's only low-calorie thali.

8 starters £3.50 such as sabudana vada (potato and sago patties), raj kachori chaat (puffed shell stuffed with moong beans and potatoes). 17 curries £7 such as the weekend special five vegetables, aloo mumraa (potato and spinach), chakki ki subzi (steamed wheat flour cakes in spicy sauce), mangodi methi (dried lentil balls cooked with fenugreek). 12 Kadhi lentil based dishes £5.

Lots of breads £3.50, and rices £5 including khichadi, a kind of porridge dish made by cooking rice with lentils, which goes well with a spicy curry.

10 desserts £3.50, vegan by request.

Typical Rajasthani drinks such as Thandai, or Shikanji Indian style lemonade. In the evening they have New World and Indian wines, beers and liquors. House wine £12.95 bottle, £3.15 glass. Kingfisher and Cobra beer from £2.65.

The basement dining room houses Indian artefacts for sale.

If you like this you should probably take a holiday in Rajasthan because you won't find anywhere else like it in London.

Eat & Two Veg

*British and International
vegetarian restaurant*

Open:

Mon-Sat 08.00–23.00
Sat   09.00–23.00
Sun   10.00–22.30

MC, Visa, Diners, Amex
Smoking permitted.
www.eatandtwoveg.com

50 Marylebone High Street
(north end), London W1U 5HN

Tel: 020-7258 8595

Tube: Baker Street
Free parking from 6.30pm
nearby and all day Sunday.
See map on page 67

Excellent new British style vegetarian restaurant and extensive bar that has been getting rave reviews from both veggies and carnivores alike. Open all day every day for breakfast, lunch and dinner with an international menu plus traditional British favourites. Your non-veggie friends will love the fake meat dishes such as full English cooked breakfast with veggie sausages, sausage and mash, burgers, shepherd's pie, and fruit crumble. Vegan dishes are clearly marked. There are lots of cocktails, juices, smoothies and wines.

Continental or full English veggie breakfast £1.50 to £7.50, served till noon Mon–Fri and till 2pm at weekends.

Soup of the day £4. Starters £4.95–5.59 such as crispl aromatic luck with pancakes; Thai spring rolls; Chinese dumplings; Thai satay skewers, Mezze with falafel, hummous, baba ghanoush and tabbouli.

12 pasta and main courses such as Thai green curry; Spaghetti/penne with fresh tomato and basil; all day breakfast; Lancashire hot pot; Schnitzel. Only a couple appear to be vegan but in fact more vegan versions can be arranged. 5 salads £3.00–7.95 such as poached pear, beet and toasted almonds with mixed leaves and seedless grapes. Sandwiches (served hot with coleslaw and fries or wedges) for £7.50 include burger, or satay soya protein in peanut sauce. Fill up with wedges, fries, mash, steamed brown rice, various veg, olives and roast almonds £1.50–2.50.

Half a dozen British desserts £5 include vegan fruit crumble, and they have Swedish Glace ice-cream.

House wine £11 bottle, £3 glass. Freshly made mixed juices £2.75. Smoothies £3.20. Cocktails £5.50–6.50.

Rasa

Vegetarian
South Indian restaurant

Open:

Mon–Sat 12.00–15.00,
18.00–23.00
Sun 18.00–23.00

No smoking on ground floor.
Reservations recommended.

6 Dering Street
off Oxford Street
Tel: 020 7629 1346
Tube: Oxford Circus,
Bond Street
MC, Visa, Amex
See map on page 67

South Indian restaurant on two floors, specialising in Keralan cuisine. Separate vegetarian and omnivorous kitchen areas. It used to be completely vegetarian, then downstairs only, and today all the veggie dishes remain the same with their own section on the menu.

Take-away Rasa Express lunchbox £2.95.

A la carte pre meal snacks £4 include nibbles made from root vegetables, rice, coconut milk, flour, lentils and seeds all beautifully spiced. Four starters, £4.25, or have a Rasa Platter £9.90 selection of starters for two people. Six pickles and chutneys £2.50. Two soups £4.25.

Three types of dosas £9.95.

Six main courses all £6.25, and five side dishes £5.25, such as vegan cheeraparippu curry with fresh spinach and toot dal.

Four kinds of rice £3–£3.75, five varieties of bread £2.50.

Several desserts include banana dosa (vegan) £3.50, mango sorbet £2.75

Wine from £10.95 bottle, £2.75 glass. Champagne £26.95 or £35. Cobra beer £2.75–4.50. Soft drinks £1.50.

Children welcome though no children's portions.

12.5% optional service charge

If you like this you'll probably like their other branch in Stoke Newington (North London) which is completely vegetarian.

Bean Juice

Cafe and juice bar

10a St Christopher's Place
London W1
Tel: 020-7224 3840

Open: *Mon-Fri* 07.30-19.30
      Sat 10.30-18.30
      Sun 11.00-18.30

Tube: Bond Street

Mostly vegetarian cafe and take-away up a small alley opposite Bond Street tube. Fresh juices, smoothies, coffees, milk shakes (can be soya), sandwiches and salads, hot soups (Sept-June). Cookies, brownies, home-made coconut cake, some vegan. No smoking except at outside tables.

Chor Bizarre

Omnivorous Indian restaurant

16 Albemarle Street, London W1
Tel: 020-7629 9802

Open: *Every day* 12.-15.00,
      18-23.30 (Sun 22.30)
Tube: Green Park

www.chorbizarrerestaurant.com
chorbizarrelondon@
oldworldhospitality.com

Big and very upmarket Indian restaurant with quite a bit of vegetarian food, though not vegan desserts. Fully licensed. Pre-theatre dinner £11 for two courses, £18 for four. Take-away dishes £6.50-9.00. Party room with bar for 10 to 35 people or bok the whole restaurant for £18 per person. Book for Sat/Sun lunch £15 and one child per adult eats free.

Levant

Omnivorous Lebanese restaurant

76 Wigmore Street, London W1
Tel: 020-7224 1111

Tube: Bond Street

One of several Lebanese restaurants just past Bean Juice, with lots for veggies.

Holland & Barrett

Health food shop

78 Baker St, London W1M 1DL
Tel: 020-7935 3544

Open: *Mon-Fri* 8.30-18.00
      Sat 9.30-17.30
      Sun closed
Tube: Baker Street

Medium sized branch with some take-away food.

Unit C12, West One Shopping Centre corner of Davis St & Oxford St,
Tel: 020-7493 7988

Open: *Mon–Fri* 08.00–19.00
Sat 09.00–19.00
Sun 11.00–17.00

Tube: Bond Street

In the Bond St tube shopping complex downstairs. Larger than usual selection of take-away savouries including sandwiches and vegan pasties and pies.

---

104 Marylebone High Street,
London W1
Tel: 020-7935 8412

Open: *Mon–Fri* 9.00– 19.00
Sat 9.00– 18.00
Sun 12.00–17.00

Tube: Baker Street

Formerly a GNC store, now taken over like all the others by Holland & Barrett, this is a small shop with basic whole-foods, snacks, but no fridge.

Leaves of Life

Vegan health and cookery classes

The Advent Centre
39 Brendon Street, W1
(corner of Crawford Place)
Tel: 020-8881 8865

Open: *Weekend seminars*

Tube: Edgware Road,
Marble Arch

Vegan health seminars and cookery classes. Email leavesoflife@aol.com for details or call. See also Local Groups at the end of this guide.

Wagamama

Omnivorous Japanese restaurant

101A Wigmore St,
London W1H 9AB
Tel: 020 7409 0111

Open: *Mon–Sat* 12.00–23.00
Sun 12.30–22.30
(last order 22.20)

Tube: Marble Arch, Bond St

Large omnivorous Japanese fast food noodle restaurant, this was the third to open in London.

See Bloomsbury, WC1 branch for menu. (page 51)

TOTTENHAM COURT RD Central London

Tottenham Court Road is the place to go for anything electronic. Whilst it has a Sainsbury's and some cafes, the real veggie action is to be found in the side-streets.

In Torrington Place, down the side of Barclays Bank, you'll find Planet Organic wholefood supermarket with a veggie cafe. One of the best things about this place is that it is open on Sundays. Another good thing is that you can buy several veggie guides here.

On the other side of Tottenham Court Road are a couple of bargain all-you-can-eat Chinese vegan buffet restaurants, Joi in Percy Street and Wai on Goodge Street, just past Tesco Metro. Nearby is a handy fruit stall in front of Goodge Street underground.

For London's best veggie sandwich selection, go right to the north end to Health Food Centre by Warren Street station, see the Euston section.

Map labels:
EUSTON (SEE MAP P52)
EUSTON ROAD
WARREN ST
Fruit & veg stall
← Health Food Centre p.54
BLOOMSBURY (SEE MAP P46)
Planet Organic p.75
Fruit & veg stall
GOODGE ST.
Wai p.76 →
Adonis p.77 →
Peppercorn's p.77
Joi p.76
Rasa Express p.76
Sainsbury's
TOTTENHAM CT.RD.
SOHO (SEE MAP P22)
OXFORD STREET
COVENT GARDEN (SEE MAP P36)

Planet Organic

Organic supermarket and vegetarian cafe

Open:

Mon–Fri	9.00–20.00
Sat	11–18.00
Sun	12–18.00

Kids welcome
MC, Visa
No smoking

22 Torrington Place
London WC1A 7JE
Tel: 020-7436 1929
Tube: Goodge St

See map on page 74

Organic wholefood supermarket off Tottenham Court Road, with a juice bar and café. Most dishes, snacks and cakes have ingredients displayed and if they're gluten, sugar free or vegan.

The deli/cafe at the front has hot and cold dishes and salads, mostly vegan, for take-away or eat in at the tables by the tills and outside. Box of food £3, £4 or £5. Cakes and flapjacks, more of which are now dairy-free. Lots of juices and smoothies £2.50–3.00 including different kinds of soya milk.

The shop sells everything for veggies including 20 types of tofu and tempeh, fake meat, every kind of pasta you can imagine and some you can't (spelt, quinoa) as well as lots of macrobiotic products for home sushi.

All organic fruit and veg.

Huge section devoted to health and body care, including vitamins, herbs, tinctures, floral essences, homeopathy, aromatherapy oils, shampoos and conditioners, sun cream.

Staff are well-trained to deal with customer queries and have in depth knowledge of what's what.

A great place for presents like pretty candles and incense. Chocolate and other treats.

They have magazines and books including Vegetarian Guides.

If you like this you'll probably like their other stores in Westbourne Grove (West London) and the new one in Fulham (Sloane Zone).

Joi

Vegan Oriental Restaurant

14 Percy Street
off Charlotte Street, London W1

Tel: 020-7323 -0981

Open: *Mon–Sat* 12-22.30
Sun 13-22.00

Tube: Goodge Street,
Tottenham Court Rd

Cash only. No smoking.

Chinese vegan buffet restaurant specialising in fake meats and run by a relative of the proprietor of Tai in Greek Street. Eat-as-much-as-you-like buffet £5 daytime, £6 evening and Sunday. Choose from chow mein, rice, sweet and sour veg "pork" balls, soya chicken, fake beef, crispy seaweed, fried aubergine, spring rolls, tofu and many more.

Desserts £2.50 such as banana or apple fritter, lychees, soya ice-cream.

No wine but you can bring your own.

£10 minimum in the de luxe area at the back. £3 or £4 for a take-away box.

Wai

Vegan Chinese restaurant

32 Goodge Street, London W1

Tel: 020 7637 4819

Open: *Every day* 12-23.00

Tube: Goodge Street

Chinese vegan buffet restaurant and take-away. Open every day for lunch and dinner. All you can eat £5, £6 after 6pm and Sunday. Take-away box £3 or £4 large.

Rasa Express

Veggie & fish Indian

5 Rathbone Street
Off Oxford Street, London W1

Tel: 020-7637-02229

Open: *Mon–Sat* 12-15.00 buffet

Tube: Tottenham Court Rd

Unlike their restaurant on the other side of the building in parallel Charlotte Street, here most of the menu is veggie snacks and take-aways.

Typical snacks for £1.50 are Mysore potato balls with ginger curry leaves, coriander and black mustard seeds, fried in chickpea flour; or crispy spongy dumpling in a crunchy case made from urad beans and chillies, with coconut chutney. Wine £2.75 glass, £11 bottle.

Take-aways £2-£2.50 such as masala dosa (vegetable stuffed pancake)

Peppercorn's

Wholefood shop

2 Charlotte Place, London W1

Tel: 020-7631 4528
Open: *Mon-Sat* 9.00-18.30
     Sat 11.00-18.00
     Sun closed
Tube: Goodge Street

10% discount for Vegetarian or Vegan Society

Organic wholefood store selling everything for veggies including tofu and tempeh, every kind of pasta and health food.

Take-away and macrobiotic specialities from around the world, some organic, with lots of vegan options including Mexican bean slices, vegetarian rotis, country pies, vegetarian sushi, spinach filo pastries, tofu parcels, rice rolls, organic hummous, cottage pies, veggie sausages, rice and curry, cakes and flapjacks. Most dishes, snacks and cakes have ingredients displayed and if they're gluten, sugar free or vegan.

Also supplements, vitamins and minerals, plus Ecover cleaning products.

Staff are well trained and have in depth knowledge of what's what.

Adonis

Lebanese omnivorous restaurant

56 Goodge Street,
London W1T 4NB
Tel: 020-7637-7687
Open: *Mon-Sat* 10.30-23.30
Tube: Goodge Street

Several vegan starters from £3 including tabbouleh salad, stuffed vine leaves, okra, eggplant and falafel. One vegetarian main dish-aubergine, okra or green beans stew served with rice, £6.90. Freshly squeezed juices from £2.

CITY Central London

The Square Mile of the financial capital still has its John Steed lookalikes sporting pinstriped suits and brollies, though these days you're more likely to see smartly dressed young and not so young men and women heading for the gym or a healthy lunch, as fitness clubs and multicultural food continue to expand and thrive in London.

From noon till 2pm there's a feeding frenzy in take-away specialists such as Futures!, Fresh & Wild, or newcomers Tiffin Bites and Pure, or treat yourself to a sit-down lunch at The Greenery or The Place Below.

For an altogether more relaxing experience on the quieter City fringes, Rye Wholefoods has a peaceful café within their shop, whilst Antimony Balance has added a juice bar in theirs.

At night the City can feel eerily empty, but you can still enjoy a feast at Chinese buffet restaurant CTB in Leather Lane or a three course meal at vegetarian restaurant Carnevale.

ISLINGT
(SEE MAP |

BLOOMSBURY
(SEE MAP P90)

Wheatley's p.84

Rye Whole p.87

CTB p.85

FARRINGDON

Leather Lane Market p.88

Antimony Balance p.82

The Gr p.

Wagamama p.86

BLACKFRIARS

RIVER

SOUTH BA
(SEE MAP F

TON
(P90)

CITY ROAD

LEVER STREET

Fresh & Wild p.88

efoods

OLD ST.

BATH STREET
BUNHILL ROW
CITY RD.

Carnevale p.80

OLD STREET
WHITECROSS STREET
ALDERSGATE

EAST END
(SEE MAP P90)

Tiffin Bites p.86

CHISWELL STREET

ARBICAN

Barbican Centre

Greenery p.84

Beech Street

Tiffin Bites p.86

MOORGATE

Pure p.83

LONDON WALL

LIVERPOOL ST.

T. PAULS

ST. PAULS STREET

t. Pauls thedral

CHEAPSIDE

Place Below p.81 St. Mary-le-Bow church

Tiffin Bites p.86

Holland & Barrett p.88

BANK

BISHOPSGATE

VICTORIA

MANSION HOUSE

PPER

Tiffin Bites p.86

CANNON ST.

Bank DLR

EASTCH

MONUMENT

THAMES ST.

LOWER THAMES ST.

SOUTHWARK BRIDGE

LONDON BRIDGE

Futures! p.85

HAMES

ANK
(90)

The Place Below

Carnevale

Mediterranean vegetarian restaurant and deli

Open:

Mon–Fri	10.00–22.30
Sat	17.30–22.30
Sun	closed

Children welcome (no high chairs) If you ask they can keep an area smoke free. Visa, MC.

135 Whitecross St.
London EC1Y 8JL

Tel: 020–7250 3452

Tube: Old Streeet, Barbican, Moregate

www.carnevalerestaurant.co.uk

See map on page 79

Vegetarian restaurant, snack bar and take–away with a glass roofed area out back. Near the Barbican Centre and Museum of London.

Set menu £13.50 (3 courses, or 2 courses and a drink): for example soup of the day; risotto with giroles, mascarpone and herbs; plum and almond tart..

A la carte starters include vegan soup of the day £3.75; warm salad with chestnut mushrooms, baked plum tomatoes and baby spinach £5.50; roasted aubergines tossed in Romesco sauce £5.50; watercress, fennel, orange and kalamata olive salad £5; celeriac and horse-radish spring rolls with mustard dressing £4.95.

Deli plate (lunchtimes only) £5.50 / £9.50.

Main courses £11.50 such as potato and shallot panisse with fennel, red pepper and flageolet beans; butternut squash Thai curry with spiced tofu balls and pak choi.

Five puddings £4.95 with vegan options including baked stuffed quince with cardamon cream; home made prickly pear sorbet with spiced poached pears.

House wine £10.95 bottle, £2.95.glass. Organic wines from £14.75/£3.95.

Minimum food order £5.50 per person. Luxury hampers from £25.65.

If you like this you'll probably like Manna in Hampstead (North London) or 222 in West London which also offer gourmet vegetarian and vegan dining.

The Place Below

Veggie restaurant & take-away

Open:

Mon–Fri 07.30–15.30,
lunch 11.30–14.30

Children welcome

MC, Visa

Non Smoking

Crypt of St Mary-le-Bow Church
Cheapside, London EC2V 6AU

Tel: 020-7329 0789

Tube: St Paul's

www.theplacebelow.co.uk

See map on page 79

Located in the Norman Crypt of a Wren church, this large vegetarian restaurant provides a quiet retreat. 80 seats inside plus 40 in the churchyard. Global food, especially Mediterranean and Middle Eastern. Menu changes daily.

Breakfast (vegan friendly) from 07.30. They make their own granola, muesli £1.80, organic porridge £1.50, muffins £1.30, croissants £1.50, fresh fruit, freshly squeezed orange juice £1.75–1.95 and Illy coffee which Italian customers say is the best in the world.

Soup £3.10 eat in, take-away £2.70. Salads £7.50 eat in, £6.20 take-away, such as tabouleh, lemon spiced carrots, aubergine puree and marinated green beans in tomato dressing.

The hot dish of the day £7.00 in, £5.70 out, might be ratatouille with Asian flavours, spiced chickpeas and coconut rice. £2 discount on dish of the day 11.30–12.00.

Healthbowl £5.50 containing wholegrain rice, puy lentils, vegetables, leaves, herbs and soy balsamic dressing.

Desserts like apple, raspberry and almond cake, £2.80 in or £2.20 to go, or fruit salad.

Special morning deal 7.30–11.30a.m.: any hot drink including soyaccinos, hot chocolate, teas and lattes for 80p a cup.

Buffet available for private hire evenings such as weddings and christenings.

Antimony Balance

Wholefood shop and juice bar

Open:

Mon–Fri	08.00–19.00
Sat	10.00–16.00
Sun	closed

47 Farringdon Road
London EC1M

Tel: 0870-3600 345

Tube: Farringdon

See map on page 79

Big wholefood store with lots of bodycare products, take-away foods and a new organic juice bar.

Big range of take-away food and tables in a cafe area coming early 2005.

One of London's best stocked wholefood stores. Extensive range of vitamins and supplements. Extensive ranges of herbal teas.

Bodycare includes Dr Hauschka, Neal's Yard, Barefoot Botanicals, Birds Bees, Weleda, Spizia Organics.

Natural gifts include aromatherapy goodies, candles, incense, lavender wheat bag hot/cold compresses.

Big range of vegetarian health and diet books.

Also veggie sandwiches, pies and pastries, nuts and seeds and delicious flapjacks.

All organic juice bar with extensive range of combinations £2.50-3.50. Shots £1.50 include wheat grass, spirulina, echinacea. Smoothies. In winter hot offerings such as miso soup.

A homeopath and nutritionist are sometimes available.

If you like this you'll probably like Bumblebee in North London, which also sells just about everything and has nice take-away food.

Pure

Vegetarian take-away

Open:

Mon–Fri	06.00–22.00
Sat	07.30–18.00
Sun	07.30–15.00

In one of the entrances of Moorgate tube at the corner of Moor Place and Moorfields, opposite Dixons electrical store.

Tel: 020-7588 7800

Tube: Moorgate

See map on page 79

Fabulous new vegetarian take-away with an astonishing range of food, most of it vegan. It's much better than JJ's which used to be nearby but has closed. There is a fridge with wraps and boxes of food, a counter with salads and hot food you can choose from, and a huge range of fresh juices and smoothies. Open long hours from dawn till late during the week.

Falafel with hummous and avocado (or tabouleh, or grilled veg) in wheat-free pitta £3.20.

Box of food £4.35 can contain grilled veg, hummous and avocado; veg curry with rice; moussaka; lentils with rice. Low fat, gluten and wheat free.

10 salads £3.75 include wild rice with grilled veg; country veg with pasta, beans and lentils; heart of palm with brown and red rice, sweet corn, chickpeas and vine leaves; Moroccan with dates.

Six kinds of wraps, white £4.10, brown £4.35, gluten free.

Soups £2.95, £3.45, £3.75.

10 kinds of fresh veg juices, 16 fruit juices and 10 smoothies £3.40, £3.95, £4.45, £4.95. Many coffees and teas £1.10-2.35.

Vegans beware of egg in all the muffins, but you could have a fruit salad for dessert.

Breakfast porridge £1.85–2.50 with raisins or banana, served with fresh fruit (strawberry, blueberry, pineapple, raspberry). Gluten free tropical or fruit and nut muesli, puffed rice cereal, porridge or wholegrain bread.

If you like this you'll probably like some of the take-away food stalls in Spitalfields Market, weekday lunchtimes and Sun morning and early afternoon.

The Greenery

Vegetarian café & take-away

5 Cowcross St
London EC1M 6DR
Tel: 020-7490 4870
Open: *Mon-Fri* 7.00-17.00.
     Sat-Sun closed
Tube: Farringdon

Busy wholefood vegetarian café with big take-away trade near Farringdon tube, with a juice bar. 50% vegan.

Breakfast with muesli, croissant, fruit scones, chocolate croissant, toast etc.

Soup £1.60 small, £2.90 large. Filled baps £1.80-£2.10. 10 salads £1.90-£3.90.

Mains like Homity pie, pasta, curries, veggie satay. £2.20-£3.75 take-away, £4.25 eat in, £5.50 with salad platter.

Desserts are mostly cakes plus fruit salad.

Fresh juices and smoothies £1.40-3.50 and they have soya milk.

You can email your order through before 11am to thegreenery@amserve.ne

Nominated for top 6 in Vegetarian Society Best Restaurant Awards 2003-4.

Wheatley's

Vegetarian café

33-34 Myddleton Street,
London EC1R 1UA
Tel: 020-7278-6662
Open: *Mon-Fri* 8.00-16.00
Tube: Angel, then 38 or 341 bus

Veggie family run café with friendly vegetarian proprietors Jane and mum, not far from Saddlers Wells. There is garden with canopy for summer showers and heaters in winter. Plenty for vegans.

Soup £2.30. Sandwiches £2.95 made to order. Around 15 salads, small £2.75, medium £3.50, large £5.00.

Many hot lunch possibilities around £3.95 including tortillas, savoury crepes and falafel wraps.

Vegan cakes £2.20.

Freshly squeezed juices, smoothies, herbal teas

Seating outside for 15, inside for about 10. They welcome parties and office lunches.

Futures!

Vegetarian take away

8 Botolph Alley
Eastcheap, London EC3R 8DR
Tel: 020-7623 4529

Open: Mon–Sat breakfast
07.30–10.00,
lunch: 11.30–15.00

Tube: Monument
Cash only

Vegetarian take-away only, in a pedestrianised alley in the heart the City. Haps for vegans.

Soup of the day £2.10. Choose from several hot dishes £4 like the bake of the day, fusilli with spinach and mushroom in a tomato and basil sauce, or stir fry veg with rice.

Four salads such as mixed bean; cabbage, apple and raisin with grain mustard dressing; mixed leaves, cucumber, mustard and cress with dill dressing. £1.30 single portion, £3 combos.

Desserts £1.80 include apricot Bakewell tart.

Smoothies sold here as well as tea, coffee and juices.

Daily changing menu emailed out nightly to 200 companies and city tycoons can check it on the website then order by phone. Orders over £15 delivered.

Parties and outside functions catered.

http://www1e.btwebworld.com/futures1
(that's www one e)

CTB

Vegan oriental buffet

88 Leather Lane
The City, London EC1

Tel: 020-7242-6128

Open: Mon–Sat 12.00–22.00
Sun closed

Tube: Farringdon. Bus 55, 243

Completely vegetarian and vegan oriental buffet restaurant in the heart of the city. All you can eat for £5.00 (all day) or you can have a take-away box for £3 or £4. Typical dishes include veg Thai curry, sweet and sour veg balls, lemon grass pot, spring rolls, crispy aubergine and black bean with mixed veg, seaweed spiced aubergine, several tasty veg curries with tofu and all kinds of fake meats.

They are licensed for alcohol.

Tiffin Bites

Indian cafe and take-away

22-23 Liverpool Street
London EC2M 7PD
Tel: 0800-505 3059

Open: *Mon–Fri* 06.30–22.00
Sat–Sun 11.00–17.00

Tube: Liverpool Street

---

122 Cannon Street
London EC4N 5AX
Tel: 0800-505 3057

Open: *Mon–Fri* 07.00–18.00
Sat–Sun closed

Tube: Cannon Street

---

24 Moorfield
London EC2Y 9AA
Tel: 0800-505 3058

Open: *Mon–Fri* 06.30–21.30
Sat–Sun closed

Tube: Moorgate

Kiosk 5, Broadgate Circle
London EC2
Tel: 020-7374 4541

Open: *Mon–Fri* 11.00–21.00
Sat–Sun closed

Tube: Liverpool Street

---

www.tiffinbites.com

New chain of omnivorous cafe style Indian places with lots of vegetarian offerings. LIght, healthy Indian foods rather than the usual lager and curry. No ghee, no colouring, GM free.

Main course tiffinboxes include vegetable biryani, chana masala and jeera aloo baked potato wedges £5.29. Gujarati daal, potato bhaji and steamed rice £4.64. Smokey aubergine, black eye bean thoran and lemon rice £4.64. Snacks £1.50 such as 3 samosas, 3 onion bhajis, 3 bateta wada, or 3 hara bara kebab. Tiffin dinner for one £5 with one tiffin box and two snacks; dinner for two £10 with two boxes and four snacks. Family feast £25 with four boxes, 8 snacks, 4 sweets (none vegan that we could see) and 4 naans.

Wagamama

Japanese omnivorous restaurant

1a Ropemaker Street,
London EC2V 0HR
Tel: 020-7588 2688

Open: *Mon–Fri* 11.30–22.00
Sat–Sun closed

Tube: Moorgate

---

109 Fleet Street
(between Farrington St & Poppins Ct)
London EC4A 2AB
Tel: 020-7583 7889

Open: *Mon–Fri* 11.30–23.00
Sat–Sun closed

Tube: Blackfriars, St Paul's

---

22 Old Broad Street
London EC2N 1HQ
Tel: 020-7256 9992

Open: *Mon-Fri* 11.30-22.00
Sat-Sun closed

Tube: Liverpool Street

2b Tower Place(by Tower of
London), London EC2Y 9AA
Tel: 020-7283 5897

Open: *Mon-Sat* 11.30-21.00
Sun 12.30-21.00

Tube: Tower Hill

---

30 Queen Street
London EC4R 1BR
Tel: 020-7248 5766

Open: *Mon-Fri* 11.30-22.00
Sat-Sun closed

Tube: Mansion House
www.wagamama.com

We're not padding the book
out, these are handy when
veggie restaurants are closed
or your mates veto them. For
menu see Bloomsbury (page
51), or check the website.

Fruit and Veg stall

Market stall

Liverpool Street Station
Open: Open every day all day
Tube: Liverpool Street

By the ticket barriers going
into the underground inside
the mainline train station.

Rye Wholefoods

Wholefood store and cafe

35a Mydletton Street,
London EC1R (off Rosebery Ave
near Sadlers Wells)
Tel: 020-7278 5878

Open: *Mon-Fri* 9.00-18.00
Sat 10.00-17.00
Sun closed

Tube: Angel

Wholefood store containing a
cafe and take-away.

Vegetarian hot dishes and
salads, mostly vegan, with
vegan dressings. Soup small
£1.35, large £1.95 take-
away, eat in £1.60-2.50.

Mixed salads, stir-fries, eat
in £1.90 medium, £2.85
large; take-away £1.55,
£2.60, £3.50. Spinach
pakora or vegan rissole
£1.10, pasties £1.39. Vegan
sandwiches £1.89, wraps
from £1.69.

Brownies 85p, cakes fom £1
and vegan ones on the way
as we go to press.

Teas 60-70p, coffee and
alternatives like barleycup,
filter 85p, hot choc £1.

Huge range of wholefoods in
a small space, flapjacks,
biscuits, vitamins, body care.

Holland & Barrett

Healthfoods & wholefoods store

139-140 Cheapside
London EC2V 6BJ
Tel: 020-7600-7415

Open: *Mon-Fri* 8.00-18.00
    Sat-Sun closed

This small store packs a lot in. Nibbles such as dried fruit and nuts, also vegan chocolate, flapjacks, supplements also some toiletries, toothpaste and chiller cabinet with vegan yogurts.

Fresh and Wild

Wholefoods store

194 Old Street,
The City London, EC1V 9FR
Tel: 020-7250 1708

Open: *Mon-Fri* 9.30-19.30
    Sat   10.30-17.30
    Sun   closed

Tube: Old St.

Large wholefood store selling a huge range of organic fruit & veg, herbs, veggie/vegan wine and beer, cosmetics, toiletries, books, vitamins and herbal remedies.

Lots of take-away snacks and sandwiches, pies, wraps, cakes. Hot soup £2.45 small or £3 large. Self-serve salad bar £2.25-3.99. Many items vegan.

Big noticeboard advertising local events.

Regular sampling sessions like skin-care ranges and new product tasting.

Above the store is the Open Centre, which has alternative therapies, workshops and talks. Flyers for practitioners and events are in the store.

Leather Lane Market

Street market

Leather Lane, EC1
Open: *Mon-Fri* 10.30-14.30
Tube: Farringdon,
    Chancery Lane

Fruit and veg, clothing and household goods.

Lush Liverpool St Stn.

Cruelty-free cosmetics

Unit 55, Broadgate Link
Liverpool St Station,
London EC2M 7YP
Tel: 020-7247 6983

Open: *Mon-Fri* 09.00-17.00
Tube: Oxford Circus

Hand-made cosmetics, 70% vegan.

VEGETARIAN
EUROPE
by Alex Bourke

"This travel guide covers the top 48 destinations in Europe - where to stay and where to eat - and is an ideal springboard for that European holiday you always wanted to take, but were unsure about the food." - **The Vegetarian Society**

"A wacky guide to the best vegetarian eateries. If eating in, take some tips on urban foraging for ingredients. Veggie Vocab lists phrases to help you shop." - **The Times**

The Euroveggie comprehensive guide
300 scrumptious vegetarian restaurants, cafes and take-aways in 48 cities in 23 countries.

Top weekend destinations + tourist hotspots
Amsterdam, Athens, Barcelona, Brussels, Copenhagen, Dublin, London, Moscow, Paris, Prague...

In depth reviews
by researchers who live in the cities.

Totally independent
no restaurant pays to be in the guide.

Vegetarian Guides

From UK and USA bookshops, £9.99, $16.95

NORTH LONDON

STOKE NEWINGTON North London

The vegetarian republic of Stoke Newington is one of the bes
areas to live if you're into cruelty free living. Although not on th
tube, it's smack in the middle of north London and quite easy t
get to by train or bus. There are some excellent parks nearby.

Stoke Newington Church Street has a huge Fresh & Wild store an
lots of great eateries of which the Keralan Indian vegetarian Ras
is our favourite. The Dervish is the newest place, family run with
delicious Turkish meze.

Higher Taste – The ultimate in veggie sweet shops!

Newington Green has excellent East Mediterranean grocers fo
hummus, baba ganoush aubergine dip, olives, flatbreads etc an
even a Turkish vegetarian patisserie and café. Two Figs café an
shop has had a change of owners and name to Pilgrims but sti
provides great veggie fare.

STOKE
NEWINGTON

CAVENOVE RD.

ABNEY PARK
CEMETERY
Yum Yum p.97
Fresh & Wild p.95
Clicia p.97
CHURCH ST.
Rasa p.94
Shamsudeen p.96
The Dervish p.98

Food For
All p.96

STOKE NEWINGTON HIGH ST.

STOKE
NEWINGTON

CLISSOLD PARK

STOKE NEWINGTON

ABNEY
ROAD

Mother Earth p.99

GREEN

LANES

ALBION

HIGHBURY

HACKNEY
(SEE EAST)

Higher Taste p.97

Pilgrims p.96

NEWINGTON GREEN RD.

NEWINGTON
GREEN

BERESFORD RD.

CANONBURY

BALLS

POND

ROAD

DALSTON
KINGSLAND

ESSEX RD.

SOUTHGATE RD.

ISLINGTON
(SEE MAP P120)

Rasa

*Vegetarian
Indian restaurant*

Open:

Sun-Thu 18-22.45
Fri-Sat 18-23.30 (last orders)

Kids welcome, but no high chairs.
Visa, MC, Diners, Amex
No smoking
Optional service charge 12.5%

55 Church Street,
Stoke Newington,
London N16 0AR

Tel: 020-7249 0344

Tube: Stoke Newington BR
Bus 476 from Angel

See map on page 93

One of London's top vege-tarian restaurants and great for parties. Rasa means taste, and not only of the food. Here you experience a taste of Kerala's villages and dishes from other south Indian states. The atmos-phere is relaxed with classic Indian music in the back-ground, with pink walls and tablecloths. Dishes that don't seem vegan can be veganized.

Starters £2.75–£3.00 such as banana boli with plaintain slices in a batter of rice and chickpea flour, seasoned with black sesame seeds and served with peanut and ginger sauce; medhu vadai spongy urad bean and chilli dumpling. Two soups such as peppery lentil broth with garlic, tomatoes, spices and tamarind.

Main courses feature a large dosa (stuffed pancake) selection and over nine curries from £5.00.

Salad and side dishes £3.45–4.00 like Kerala salad of guava, avocadoes, stir-fried Indian shallots, fresh coconut, lemon juice and chilli powder; vendakka thoran of fresh okra fried with shallots, garlic, chillis, mustard seeds and curry leaves; kovakki olathiathu with tindori (like baby cucumbers), cashew nuts dry roasted with coconut mustard seeds and curry leaves. 6 kinds of rice from £2.

Desserts £2.20-3.00 include vegan ice-cream and mango halva.

Kerala feast £15.50 per head with pre-meal snacks, starters, curry selection, side dishes, breads and a tradi-tional Keralan sweet.

House wine from £8.95 bottle, £2.50 glass.

If you like this then try their other branch in Dering Street (see Marylebone, Central London). The other Rasa in N16 opposite isn't vegetarian.

Fresh and Wild

Wholefood supermarket, vegetarian cafe and juice bar

Open:
Summer
Mon–Sat 18.30–22.45
Sun   09–20.30
Winter
Mon–Sat 09–21.00
Sun   10–20.00

32–40 Church St,
Stoke Newington,

Tel: 020 7249 0344

Tube: Stoke Newington BR
              Bus 476 from Angel
              106 from Finsbury Park
See map on page 93

Huge health food shop and café concentrating on organic produce. Offering a large range of veggie and vegan food, although they do sell a small amount of meat and fish.

The café seats around 15 people and serves until about ten minutes before the store closes. Serve-yourself salad bar, deli section with hot food, and another section dedicated to cakes where you buy coffee, soyacinno and tea. Cake ingredients are clearly labelled and usually one is vegan.

Big selection of organic fruit and veg as well as organic herb plants, organic wine, beers and ciders with clear veggie/vegan signs.

Another area is given over to all kinds of toiletries, aromatherapy oils, supplements and herbal remedies, many of which are veggie and vegan. There is usually a staff member who can advise you,

and a nearby info board displays local alternative health practitioners.

Well stocked range of books on many subjects adjacent to the toiletries counter. There is a small bulletin board at the front of the shop for local events.

***

If you like this then don't miss their other five stores in Soho (Centre), Old Street (City), Clapham (South), Westbourne Grove (West) and Camden (North).

Pilgrims

Vegetarian café and shop

101 Newington Green,
Stoke Newington, London N1
Tel: 020-7690-6811

Open: *Mon–Thu* 8.30–19.00
Fri 8.30–17.00
Sun: 10.00–17.00

Tube: Angel then 73 Bus
Or Highbury & Islington
and short walk

Veggie café and food shop.
Eat in or take away.

Around 4 salads, usually pies
or pastries, all made on the
premises. The deli has a
gourmet selection of olives
and Sicilian patés. Filled rolls
with some vegan options like
red pepper and houmous, or
veggie sausage and vegan
mayo with salad. They make
their own cakes and scones.
Plenty of herbal teas, coffees,
and cold juices.

Organic bread and gluten-
free ranges, organic baby
food. Unusual and
sometimes handmade cards,
aromatherapy oils, candles,
cruelty-free toiletries and
toothpastes. Ecover refill
service.

Shamsudeen

Omnivorous Malaysian
& South Indian restaurant

35 Church St,
Stoke Newington,London N16
(next to Fresh & Wild)

Tel: 020 7241 4171

Tube: Stoke Newington BR

Omnivorous Malaysian &
South Indian restaurant.
Vegetarian menu for two
people £22.60. Licensed.

Food For All

Vegetarian wholefood store

3 Cazenove Road,
Stoke Newington,
London N16 6PA
Tel: 020-8806 4138

Open: *Mon–Wed* 9.00–18.00
Thu–Fri 9.00–19.00
Sat 10.00–18.00
Sun: 10.00–15.00

Tube: Stoke Newington BR

Popular veggie wholefood
shop with complementary
medicine, herbs and spices.
Over 300 brands of herbal
remedies, and dried herbs
sold by weight. Great chilled
section with many vegan
cheeses and sausages. Take-
away has samosas, falafels,
kebabs, pakoras. There is a
noticeboard in the shop and

a yoga centre upstairs. Funded by the Ananda Marga charity who are involved in a lot of work helping communities and rural areas become more prosperous.

Higher Taste

Vegetarian Turkish patisserie & café

47 Newington Green
Stoke Newington, Islington
London N16 9PX
Tel: 020-7359-2338
Open: *Mon–Sat* 07.00-20.00
Sun 09.00-18.00
Tube: Highbury & Islington then
73 to Newington Green

Turkish vegetarian patisserie and café, possibly the only one in London, with seating for around fifteen people.

Vegetables stews, homemade houmous and other hot and cold dishes available.

They have lots of veggie Turkish delicacies such as savoury and sweet pastries with many fillings like potato and spinach, various cakes and Turkish style biscuits. Amazing baklavas, Turkish sweets with pistachio nuts and syrup, which have to be tasted to be believed, including honeyless ones for vegans.

Tea and coffee as well as cold drinks.

Clicia

Omnivorous cafe-grill and mezze bar

97 Church St, Stoke Newington,
London N16 0UD
(corner of Defoe Rd)
Tel: 020-7254 1025
Open: *Mon–Sun* 08.00-23.00
Tube: Stoke Newington BR

Omnivorous Turkish restaurant with 20 hot and cold veggie mezze starters £2.70-3.80. 10 mains £7.50-9.50.

Yum Yum

Omnivorous Thai restaurant

26 Church St,
Stoke Newington, London N16
Tel: 020 7254 6751
Open: *Sun–Thu* 12-3 & 6-11
Fri–Sat 12-3 & 6-11.30
Tube: Stoke Newington BR

Vegetarian set lunch main course only £4.95, with starter £6.95, including tea or coffee. Evening veg starter and main £16 per person, again includes tea or coffee.

The Dervish

Omnivorous
Turkish cafe-restaurant

Open:
Mon-Sun 09-23.00
(Fri/Sat till midnight)

Smoking allowed but front is
open. Visa, MC. Licensed.

15 Church St,
Stoke Newington, London N16
Tel: 020-7923 9999
Tube: Stoke Newington BR
Bus 476 from Angel
106 from Finsbury Park
See map on page 93

*With its bright pink facade,
it's hard to miss this new
family run Turkish restaurant opposite Fresh & Wild.*

Falafel sandwich £3.10 if you
want a quick meal. Lots of
veggie starter mezze dishes
£1.95-2.35, or £3.55 for a
platter of 7 cold and 2 hot
starters.

7 veggie mains £4.95-5.20
such as falafel with broad
beans; Imam Bayildi deli-
cately fried aubergine stir-
fried with traditional onion
mixture.

Set meal of mezze, main,
tea/coffee and dessert
£11.95 per person, minimum
two people, though after a
big starter plate of mixed
mezze you may not have
room for much else! (and a
plate of what is effectively a
big portion of one of the
mezze was a bit of an anti-
climax, how much falafel can
one person eat?)

Turkish desserts £1.60-4.40,
but none vegan.

House wine £8.95 bottle,
£3.45 glass. Liqueurs and
shorts £2.50.

If you've just come out of the
pub and missed them, you
can still get a few Turkish
veggie dishes at the
Pamukkale take-away
opposite, open right up till
5am on a Saturday night.

If you like this you'll probably like Tas
on the South Bank (Central London),
another Turkish restaurant with lots of
veggie food.

Mother Earth

Organic wholefood shop

5 Albion Parade,
Albion Road
Stoke Newington,
London N16 9LD
Tel: 020-7275 9099

Open: *Mon-Thu* 9.30-20.30
Fri 9.30-20.00
Sun: 11.00-19.00

Tube: Highbury and Islington or
Angel then 73 bus

Colourful wholefood shop with small amount of fresh organic fruit and veg, macrobiotic and organic products. They also sell veggie sausages, bread and assorted veggie snacks including some vegan cakes and pies. The freezer counter has vegan ice-cream, choc ices and fruit ice-lollies in various flavours. Cruelty-free toiletries such as shampoos, lip balms, soaps and veggie toothpaste, green/environmental magazines, small selection of books, Ecover refills. Natural remedies and friendly advice. Water purifying service. Bulk produce, weigh and pay, discount on cases.

CAMDEN
North London

Camden was once the working class district on the north-east edge of Regent's Park. These days it attracts an eclectic mix, who at the weekend flock in their thousands to London's most popular market (actually six markets) off the High Street and around the Lock, which give you the best choice of hip new and secondhand clothes in town. There are some veggie and veggie-friendly food stalls and take-aways and the Psychedelic Dream Temple vegetarian café's mushroom tea left one reader high but not dry. The arty bit around the Lock is more expensive but has an interesting range of stalls. You can buy all your presents here in one go. Throbbin' in summer.

Camden features some of the best bars, clubs and pubs in London which are the basis of a lively music scene. For a fast and good value bite beforehand try the new Healthier Eating Café or Tai Buffet. Gourmet dining is at Manna or Heartstone, or check out the veggie offerings at restaurants from many countries. Café Seventy-Nine is a more laid-back experience before or after a walk on Primrose Hill with its terrific views over London, or try the new Little Earth Cafe opposite Manna.

Primrose Hill's finest

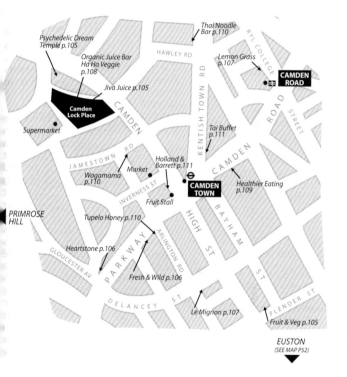

Psychedelic Dream Temple p.105

Organic Juice Bar Ha Ha Veggie p.108

Jiva Juice p.105

Thai Noodle Bar p.110

HAWLEY RD

Lemon Grass p.107

RYL COLLEGE

CAMDEN ROAD

Camden Lock Place

CAMDEN

Supermarket

KENTISH TOWN RD

ROAD

STREET

Tai Buffet p.111

JAMESTOWN RD

Market

Holland & Barrett p.111

CAMDEN

Wagamama p.110

INVERNESS ST

CAMDEN TOWN

Healthier Eating p.109

Fruit Stall

HIGH ST

BAYHAM

PRIMROSE HILL

Tupelo Honey p.110

GLOUCESTER AV

Heartstone p.106

PARKWAY

ARLINGTON RD

Fresh & Wild p.106

DELANCEY ST

Le Mignon p.107

ST

PLENDER ST

Fruit & Veg p.105

EUSTON
(SEE MAP P52)

Manna

Vegetarian restaurant

Open:

Mon–Sat 18.30–23.00
Sun 12.30–15.00
  18.30–12.30

MC, Visa. No smoking.
Children welcome. High chairs.
www.manna-veg.com

4 Erskine Road, Primrose Hill,
Hampstead, London NW3 3AJ

Tel: 020 7722 8028

Tube: Chalk Farm
Service not included.
Discretionary 12.5% added to
parties of 6 or more.

Very classy international gourmet vegetarian restaurant with lots of vegan food, set in a picturesque street near Primrose Hill, still going strong after 30 years, with incredibly friendly and efficient service by staff from all over the world. There is some seating in the conservatory and outside. The menu is constantly changing with the seasons.

Starters £3.95–6.95, include Thai glazed kebabs.

3 salads £3.95–5.95 such as crisply mock duck.

Manna Meze of any 3 starters or salads for £14.50.

Mains £10.95–12.50, half vegan, such as Tapas Olé with smoky tofu albondigas al jerez, Catalan minted broad beans, grilled sour dough panboli, spinach and carrot croquetas, garbanzo salad and orange, avocado and olive salad; or Summer

Tomato, Coconut & Ginger Curry with baby carrots, sweetcorn, mangetout and yellow courgette served with cashew rice and a sweet cucumber salsa topped with crispy noodles.

Desserts £3.95 to £6.75, plenty vegan, like petits fours, a plate of truffles, chocolates and biscuits. Organic fruit crumble, pecan chocolate cake. Vegan ice cream.

Lots of liqueurs and vegan wines. Beer from £2.60, wine £2.95 a glass or £10.50 a bottle. Organic fruit wine £9.75. Champagne £26.95, half bottle £13.95.

Kosher wine and food no problem. They even use organic soya. They serve till 11pm and it's advisable to book as not surprisingly they are very popular.

If you like this you'll probably like The Gate in Hammersmith which also serves gourmet food, desserts and wine.

Little Earth Cafe

Vegetarian organic cafe and juice bar

Open:

Mon–Fri	9–15.00, 17–20.00
Sat	10–18.00
Sun	11–15.00

No mobile phones. Non smoking. Children welcome, organic baby food.

in Triyoga Centre
6 Erskine Road
Primrose Hill, London NW3
(almost opposite Manna)

Tel: 020 7483 3344

Tube: Chalk Farm
www.triyoga.co.uk

New organic cafe in a yoga and therapies centre in Primrose Hill. Half raw, almost all vegan apart from two sandwiches. Lots of juices and smothies. An oasis of peace up the road from the bustle of Camden. Heavy emphasis on organic, raw, wheat free, yeast free, sugar free and dairy free (apart from the sandwiches), so great for vegans who have limited choice at the nearby Cafe 79.

Organic vegan raw breakfast Nutty Monkey £4 of almond butter with orange juice, ground flax seeds, sunflower seeds and thin apple slices.

Organic vegan hot food menu includes humus sandwich £3.50 with biodynamic spelt-rye bread, braised red pepper and watercress; Johnny sandwich £4 with beetroot pate, watercress, avocado, balsamic, red onion, cucumber, alfalfa and olive oil; soup £3; quinoa of the day £5.50.

Raw food menu features organic pink sushi £4; rainbow salad £4.50; almond burger £5.50 with pinenut "cheese", avocado, sprouts and cucumber relish; pizza £5.90; arame salad £5.

Raw desserts menu £3.50 has chocolate banofie, carrot cake, blue fig tart with lavender-walnut cream, blueberry cake with lemon cashew cream. Cocoa cream £1.

Organic smoothies £4 small, £5 large. Shakes and mixed juices £3-4. Spirulina shot 50p. Oganic teas £1.50.

Special juices for pregnancy and mummy. Organic baby food £1.50: avocado and banana puree or fruit smoothie pudding.

If you like this you'll probably like Organic13 (North London) or VitaOrganic (Hampstead).

Cafe Seventy Nine

Vegetarian cafe and take-away

Open:

Mon–Sat 08.30–18.00
Sun 09.00–18.00

Kids welcome, one high chair
MC, Visa
Smoking allowed only outside.

79 Regents Park Road
Primrose Hill
London NW1 8UY

Tel: 020-7586 8012
Tube: Chalk Farm

Modern vegetarian café and take-away with a small number of seats outside in one of London's most picturesque streets on the edge of Primrose Hill. Catering for the lunchtime and weekend trade predominantly.

There is an extensive menu, though vegans will find almost all of the dishes contain dairy or eggs.

All day full English cooked breakfast special £6.45. Croissants, bagels and toast £1.95.

Organic soup of the day with organic Neal's Yard roll £4.45.

Houmous and warm wholemeal pitta £3.65. Veggie burger and salad £4.45. Baked potato £2.75, or £3.95 with a filling then £1.45 per extra filling. Side salads £2.45.

Sandwiches, toasted sand-wiches, baguettes and bagels from £2.65.

Main courses such as pasta with pesto, pine nuts, cherry tomatoes and green salad £6.25.

Bagel burger and deep fried new potatoes £5.75.

Lovely big salads £6.95.

Nine kinds of cakes and desserts from £2.45, but not vegan.

Lots of teas, coffees and soft drinks, with a pot of tea for one £1.65.

Freshly squeezed orange juice £2.65.

Milkshakes £2.95, can be made with soya milk. (Soya) cappuccino £1.65–1.95.

Free corkage.

If you like this after a walk on Primrose Hill, you'll probably like Cicero's on Clapham Common or Queens Wood Weekend Cafe.

Inverness Street Market

Street market

Inverness Street,
off Camden High Street
Open: *Mon–Sat* 08.30–17.00
Tube: Camden Town

A few fruit and veg stalls, which you won't find in the main Camden markets, which are all clothes and jewellery. There's also a handy fruit stall on the corner of Parkway and Camden High Street, and a few more stalls down the High Street at the corner with Plender Street.

Jiva Juice

Juice Bar

45/46 Camden Lock
London NW1 8AF
Tel: 020 7586 8012

www.jivajuice.com

Open: *Mon–Fri* 8.00–17.00
Sat–Sun 10.00–18.00
Tube: Camden Town

New juice bar in Camden Lock Market between the Middle and West Yards. Over 20 juices and smoothies £1.80–3.70, or concoct your own. 50p more gets you a boost of aloe vera, echinacea, gingko biloba, ginseng, guarana, milk thistle or spirulina. Jacket potatoes £2–3, pasta salad £2.99, sandwiches £2.50, soups, baked potatoes, teas, bottled water 80p.

Dream Temple Cafe

Almost Vegan Cafe

Above the Dream Temple record shop, 21–22 Stables Market, Camden, London NW1 8AH
Tel: 020–7267 8528

Open: Mon–Sun 10.30–18.30
Fri–Sun 21.00–late
Tube: Camden Town

All vegan, apart from cow's milk in drinks, psychedelic café at the back of Camden Stables Market (the last one on the left going north up Camden High Street). The décor is a mix between Indian, Arabic and Morrocan, with beautiful low tables, seats and floor cushions. They also sell psychedlic, spiritual, shamanic and meditation books on the same floor, and downstairs is a world and psychedelic CD store with trancy music thumping out. It's non–smoking during the day, but you can smoke at their chill out nights Fri–Sun from 9pm until late, we mean late, could be till 02.00. "A great place to warm up for the weekend, meet friends, or to recover from your partying antics."

Organic herbal teas, Arabic tea, Moroccan tea, chai, organic coffee, (soya) latte or cappuccino, £1.30–2.00, or £3.00 for a large pot.

Smoothies £3, fresh organic hemp milk £2, organic vegan lassi £2. Also kombucha, guava drink, coconut water.

Vegan brownies, flapjacks and cakes £2.

At weekends there are vegan meals, which depending on the chef could be soups, pastries, pasta, e.g. a big bowl of soup with bread for £3 or a main meal £5.

No alcohol, no eggs. Available for private hire.

Fresh & Wild

Organic Supermarket

49 Parkway
Camden Town
London NW1 7PN
Tel: 020-7428 7575
Open: *Mon–Fri* 8.00–21.00
        Sat: 9.30–21.00
        Sun: 10.30–20.00
Tube: Camden Town

Huge organic supermarket

with a café with a few seats inside and some tables outside. The store sells everything from tea to toothpaste and has a big takeaway food and juice bar. Load up here for a day out in Regents Park or a wander to nearby fashionable Camden Lock market. Take-away food bar by weight, £1–1.50 per 100g, with lots of salads, baked tofu and savouries (not all vegetarian). Muffins and cakes, some of them vegan, and soyacinno for vegan coffee lovers. Large range of vegetarian and vegan products, the only meat is hidden in a fridge at the back. Natural remedies, bodycare, books. Great choice of organic fruit and vegetables.

Heartstone

Almost vegetarian resturant

106 Parkway
London NW1 7AN
Tel: 020 7485 7744

Open: *Tue–Sat* 8.30–21.30
        Sun   10.00–16.00

Tube: Camden Town

Upmarket mostly vegetarian wholefood organic restaurant. Soup £4.50, starters such as hummous with veg sticks £4.50, salad with avocado and alfalfa sprouts £5.50 or £9.50 as a main course. Falafel with salad £9.50. Tofu sausage sandwich £8.50. Avocado salad sandwich £8.60. Desserts £2.50-6.50. Juices, smoothies. Also massage and nutritional consultations, books, organic products. No smoking. Licensed.

Le Mignon

Omnivorous Lebanese

9a Delancey Street, corner of Arlington Rd
Camden Town
London NW1
Tel: 020 7586 8012

Open: *Tue–Sun* 12.00-15.00
　　　　　　　　18.00-24.00
　　　Mon closed

Tube: Camden Town

Sweet little Lebanese restaurant with a couple of outside tables on a quiet side street off Camden High St, round the back of Woolworths.

Like virtually all Lebanese places, main dishes are meat based and starters are vegetable based. Dairy products and eggs are rarely used. Staff are very friendly and it is clear from the menu what is veggie/vegan and what isn't.

There are around 22 hot and cold vegan starters £3.95-5.00, so if you and a friend order 3 different ones each, you can create a tasty feast.

House wine £2.50 (125ml glass) –3.00 (175ml), £11.75 bottle. Beer £2.20. MC, Visa, Amex. Smoking allowed everywhere.

Lemon Grass

Omnivorous

243 Royal College Street
Camden Town
London NW1
Tel: 020-7284 1116

Open: *Every day* 17.30-23.30
　　　　Last orders 22.30

Tube: Camden Town,
　　　Camden Road BR

Small, brightly lit and smoke-free Cambodian restaurant round the corner from Camden Road rail station. Separate vegetarian menu with mostly stir-fry dishes. Starters £3 include golden triangles of curry potato, veg spring rolls, garlic lemon mushrooms, fried leek cake with chilli sauce, or have a plate of the last 4 with ginger/shallots for 2+ people for £5 each. Mains £5 such as Buddhist cabbage with peppers, rainbow stir-fry, pak choy ginger, spicy veg. Mango or bamboo salad £3.90. Steamed rice £1.80. Desserts include fresh mango, rambutan, lychees, pineapple or banana fritters. Veg set feast £15.80 per head, minimum 2 people, of 5 treats with dips, mango salad, Buddhist cabbage, fresh asparagus or spiced veg, steamed rice, fresh mango/pineapple or lychee. Wine £2.80 glass, £11.80 bottle. MC, Visa.

Paradise Foods

Health food shop

164 Kentish Town Road
Kentish Town
London NW5
Tel: 020-7284 3402
Open: *Mon–Sat* 10.00–18.00
Tube: Kentish Town

Health food shop that stocks a wide range of unusual veggie foods from all around the world. Great selection of herbs and spices, also organic fruit and veg delivered 2–3 times a week. They have a small range of gluten-free and sugar-free foods. Organic vegetarian wheat-free sandwiches and salads, dairy free ice-cream. Some shampoos, soaps and supplmements.

Muang Thai

Omnivorous Thai Restaurant

71 Chalk Farm Road,
London NW1 8AN
(between Belmont and Ferdinand St)
Tel: 020-7916 0653
Open: *Tue–Sat* 12–15.00
every day 18.00–23.00
Tube: Chalk Farm

Thai restaurant with amazing coconut rice and garlic rice plus veggie dishes. Three doors further south at 68 is Neal's Yard Remedies.

The Ha Ha Veggie Stall

Vegetarian & vega n take away

Row of food stalls,
West Yard entrance.
Camden Lock market
Camden Town
London NW1

Open: *Sat–Sun* 10.00–17.00
Tube: Camden Town

Stall selling falafels, drinks and large, homemade veggie burgers with a range of toppings such as avocado and pineapple. All are vegan except the cheeseburger. Prices £2–3.00.

The Healthier Eating Café

Omnivorous café

24 Camden Road,
Camden Town,
London NW1 9DP
Tel: 020-7267 2649

Open: *Mon–Fri*   06.30–19.30
         Sat   08.00–20.00
         Sun   11.00–20.00

Tube: Camden Town

New, opened May 2004, offering a healheir eating meal to the general middle market. Beatiful modern design, with bright yellow frontage and interior, very light. Local artists' pictures hang on the walls. Natural wood tables, soft seating or Thai seating and the gorgeous leather look sofa isn't leather, ok vegans? There's a student crowd in the afternoons.

All food has clear labelling and brief nutrition highlights info.

Take-away salads and sandwiches £2.50-3.00 such as roast pepper with hummus and roquette with black olives. Mexican wild rice and bean salad £2 take-away, £3.50 eat in. Barley couscous with roasted Mediterranean veg £2 / £3.50.

Drinks 80p–£2.50 include smoothies made from 13 flavours of Brazilian fruits, teas, coffees, (soya) cappuccino. There's sometimes a freshly squeezed orange juice stand out front. Crayve's cakes, though none of these are vegan.

Child friendly and a small children's menu which provides nutritional info for parents.

Sesame Health Foods

Wholefood Shop

128 Regents Park Road
London NW1
Tel: 020-7586 3779

Open: *Mon–Frid*   9.00–18.00
         Sat   10.00–18.00
         Sun   12.00–17.00

Tube: Chalk Farm

Wholefoods and fresh foods. Take-away items include soups, salads, rice and vegetables, snacks, pasta, stir-fries, cakes. Organic fruit and veg. Bread comes from several different bakers. Lots of snacks. All you need for a summer picnic on nearby Primrose Hill. Natural remedies and body care.

Wagamama

Omnivorous Japanese

11 Jamestown Road,
Camden Town,
London NW1 7BW

Tel: 020-7428 0800

Open: *Mon–Sat* 11.00–23.30
Sun 12.30–22.30

Tube: Camden Town

Omnivorous fast food Japanese noodle bar with over nine veggie and vegan dishes. See Bloomsbury, WC1 branch for menu.

Thai Noodle Bar

Vegan Chinese Restaurant

81 Kentish Town Road, Camden, London

Tel: 020 7586 8012

Open: Every day

Tube: Camden Town

Opening soon after this gude goes to press and with the same formula as the new Noodle Bar already open in Islington. As there, this is in fact a specialist in Chinese dumplings and fake meats. Xiao Cai assorted cold and pickled veg £2.50, seaweed £3.50, garlic vegetable pork £3.50, five kinds of dumplings with spicy sauce £4.50–5.50.

Tupelo Honey

Omnivorous café

(corner of Arlington St)
27 Parkway, Camden, London
NW1 7PN

Tel: 020-7284 2989

Open: *Tue–Sat* 9.30–23.30
Sun 12.00–20.00
Mon 9.30–18.00

Tube: Camden Town

Popular and chilled out omnivorous café with several rooms on three floors with wooden tables, a small outside area and a roof garden. Several veggie dishes e.g. couscous, slightly curried root veg £6.95. Desserts include carrot cake. House wine £11.50 bottle, £2.85 glass, beer £2.50. Cappuccino £1.40, latte £1.60, they have soya milk. Children welcome, no high chair yet. They are opening up the basement for a chill out bar with sofas. Non-smoking ground floor, smoking upstairs. After our visit they are planning more vegan.

Tai Buffet

Vegan Chinese Restaurant

6 Kentish Town Road,
Camden, London, NW1
(just up from the tube)

Tel: 020-7284 4004

Open: Every day all day

Tube: Camden Town

Chinese vegan buffet restaurant and take-away with lots of fake meat. Open every day for lunch and dinner. All you can eat £5, £6 after 6pm and Sunday. Take-away box £3 or £4 large.

Holland & Barrett

Health food shop

55 High St, St John's Wood
London NW8 7NL

Tel: 020-7586 5494

Open: Mon-Sat   9.00-17.30
      Sun   Closed

Tube: St Johns Wood

Health food shop. This one doesn't have a freezer cabinet so no vegan ice-cream here.

191-200 High St, Camden
London NW1 0LT

Tel: 020-7485-9477

Open: Mon-Sat   8.30-18.30
      Sun   9.00-18.30

Tube: Camden Town

One of the largest London branches of this national chain. They have lots of take-away items such as pies, pastries, Mexican slices and cakes. Large range of soya milks, vegan chocolate, dried goods, ready meals, nut roasts, toiletries, supplements, non-dairy cheeses, yoghurt and ice-creams. Relaxing music CD's at the back.

ISLINGTON
North London

Gateway to north London, home of Prime Minister Tony Blair and some cracking vegetarian eateries, Islington is a somewhat swanky shopping area that's great for designer gifts, antiques and the farmers' market in Camden Market (not the one in Camden Town further west) on Upper Street.

Some shops in Chapel Market (fruit and veg) have bargain non leather jackets.

Islington offers amazing value for a veggie night out. Diners converge from all over to meet their friends at Indian Veg Bhelpuri House for the cheapest all-you-can-eat buffet in London.

Nearby in Chapel Market is a new restaurant called Chinese Veg. This is in fact omnivorous but retains a lot of vegan fake meat dishes. However for a 100% vegan Chinese feast you need to visit Tai Buffet opposite Angel underground. Next door is a new vegan noodle bar.

For something completely different, Patisserie Bliss is London's only vegetarian French pastries shop and café.

The Candid Cafe behind Angel Tube Station

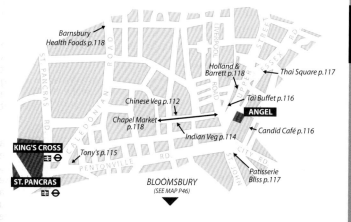

Barnsbury
Health Foods p.118

Holland &
Barrett p.118 → Thai Square p.117

Chinese Veg p.112 → Tai Buffet p.116

Chapel Market
p.118 ← ANGEL

Indian Veg p.114 ← Candid Café p.116

KING'S CROSS

Tony's p.115

ST. PANCRAS

BLOOMSBURY
(SEE MAP P46)

Patisserie
Bliss p.117

Indian Veg Bhelpuri

*Vegetarian and Vegan
Indian restaurant*

Open: *Every day:* 11.00–23.00
MC and Visa only.
Smoke free zone.
Licensed.
See map on page ?

92–93 Chapel Market
Islington
London N1 9EX
Tel: 020-7837 4607
Tube: Angel

Best value veggie restaurant in London with a great bargain all-you-can-eat-buffet that runs all day long. Fantastic value for money here on the edge of trendy Islington, where you could easily stretch your wallet beyond the total bill here by going to nearby Upper Street for just starters or a couple of drinks. Indian Veg promotes the benefits of a vegetarian diet and were serving organic brown rice long before it ever got fashionable in this part of town. Come to think of it, how many Indian restaurants can you think of that even serve it or have non-dairy lassi?

Eat as much as you like for £2.95 (the only place in this book to drop its price since the last edition) from the buffet which has 3 types of rice, 3 curries, onion bhaji, poori, 3 sauces and lentil dhal. You can go back as many times as you like.

If you prefer a la carte there are snacks and starters from £1.95 like veg kebab or brinjal (aubergine slices) deep fried in gram flour. Mains include five thalis £3.95, dosas £3.50.

One of the few Indian restaurants that will make fresh vegan lassi for you with soya or rice milk in different flavours, £2.15. Juices 99p. 14 kinds of organic fruit juice in cans £1.65. Tea 85p, herb tea 95p, coffee or cappuccino £1.60. Now serving alcohol: beers 330ml £1.99, 500ml £2.95, 710ml £3.95. Wine from £6.95 bottle, £1.95 glass.

They even some vegan desserts (other Indian restaurants please note!), and so are a popular restaurant with London Vegans.

They use vegetable oil not butter ghee.

See picture page ## (90 ish)

Tony's Natural Foods

Vegan organic cafe, shop and juice bar

Open:
Mon–Fri 09–15.00
Sat–Sun closed
No smoking.
MC, Visa.
Children welcom, no high chairs.

10 Caledonian Road
Kings Cross
London N1 9DU
Tel: 020-7837 5223
Tube: Kings Cross
See map on page 54

Bustling, very friendly vegan organic shop with juice bar and garden cafe where you can come take respite and relax beneath a great 150 yearold fig tree. Just a short walk from King's Cross station.

Different soup every day, £1.35 small take-away (£1.45 eat in), £2.40 large (£2.80).

Hot food (mostly vegan or wheat free and organic)£2.80 small take-away (£3.20 eat in), £4.50 large (£5.20), such as veg curry cooked in fresh coconut oil, mung bean stew, and red cabbage pie.

Vast selection of salads including sprouted quinoa, sunflower and hemp seeds.

Sandwiches £2.25 and hemp flour baps. Vegan cake £1.25 like apple and date or chocolate, banana and almond.

Spirulina and fruit smoothies £2.50 with freshly made nut and hemp seed milk.

Also wholefoods, supplements, hemp seed and oil (great for omega essential fatty acids) and some hemp clothing and literature on the history of hemp products and its many beneficial uses. Cruelty-free toiletries.

Medicinal cannabis and herbal remedies clinic attached with therapies like relexology, energy healing, Japanese massage. Clinic open Mon–Fri 10–18.00, Sat–Sun 11–17.00.

If you like this you'll probably like Bumblebee in the middle of North London, which also has a big selection of foods, and the nearby Eco13 shop.

Tai Buffet

Chinese vegan restaurant

13 Islington High St
Islington
London N1
Tel: 020-7837 7767

Open: *every day* 12-24.00
Fri-Sun till 01.00

Tube: Angel

Yet another new Chinese vegan eat-as-much-as-you-like buffet, right opposite Angel tube station.

£5 daytime, £6 evening, or £3 for a take-away box.

Choose from chow mein, rice, sweet and sour veg "pork" balls, soya chicken, fake beef, crispy seaweed, fried aubergine, spring rolls, tofu and many more.

They have a vegan noodle bar (more of a Chinese vegan dumpling bar) two doors down at number 11.

Candid Café

Omnivorous restaurant

3 Torrens Street
Islington
London EC1V 1NQ
Tel: 020-7278 9368

Open: *Mon-Sat* 12.00-22.00
Sun 12.00-17.00

Tube: Angel

Climb the stairs to get to this lofty arthouse style omnivorous café just behind the Angel tube station. Faded renaissance interior with red velvet and chipped gold leaf chairs, with some very interesting pieces of art work to gaze at!

Several veggie offerings like stuffed aubergine with herbs and veg for £6.00 (evening), which comes with salad. Also broccoli soup (vegan) with bread for £4.00. The menu changes daily.

Several sweets £3.50 such as cakes, but none vegan. Coffee or cappuccino £1.50, tea and herbal teas £1.30. They have soya milk. House wine £7 bottle, £2.50 glass. Beers £2.80 bottle.

Patisserie Bliss

Vegetarian French patisserie

428 St. Johns Street
Junction of Upper St. &
Pentonville Rd
Islington, London EC1V 4NJ
Tel: 020 7586 8012

Open: *Mon–Fri* 8.30–18.00
      Sat 8.30–18.00
      Sun: 9.00–16.00

Tube: Angel

Vegetarian French patisserie
and boulangerie with seating
inside and take-aways. It was
in fact the first coffee shop
with patisserie in Islington in
1989, now there are lots of
them, but this is the only
French one.

They serve a range of filled
croissants, filo parcels and
puff pastry, as well as sweet
items such as almond croissants, fruit tarts and cakes.
Unfortunately they are rather
keen on using eggs, butter
and cream so not particularly

*Bliss Cafe is the only French
vegetarian patisserie in Londres*

vegan friendly.

Various continental coffees:
cappuccino £1.50, latte
£1.60, mocha etc.

Non-smoking throughout.

Thai Square

Thai omnivorous restaurant & bar

347–349 Upper Street
Islington, London N1 0PD
Tel: 020-7704 2000

Open: *Mon–Fri* 12.00–15.00
            18.00–23.00
      Sat 12.00–23.00
      Sun 12.00–22.30

Tube: Angel

Big classy Thai restaurant
with a whole page of veggie
dishes. 6 starters £3.95–
4.55 like tempura, fried bean
curd, crispy seaweed, corn
cake with sweet chilli sauce,
or have a mixed selection
£10.95 for two people. 3
soups £4.25–4.45.

8 main courses £6.25–6.95
such as green or red or hot
curry, stir-fry, fried bean
curd, steamed vermicelli. £1
for extra bean curd. Rice
sticky, steamed or with
coconut £1.90–2.50. Extra
veg £4.50.

House wine £9.95 bottle,
£2.95 glass. Soft drinks

£1.50–3.00. Liqueurs, spirits, lots of wines up to £23.50, champagne from £16.50.

Smoking area. MC, Visa. www.Thaisq.com

Holland & Barrett

Health food shop

212 Upper Street
Islington, London N1 1RL

Tel: 020-7226 3422

Open: *Mon–Sat* 9.00–19.00,
Sat 9.00–18.00
Sun 12–17.00

Tube: Highbury and Islington

Take–away section with sandwiches and snacks, vegan pastries including Mexican bean slice and veggie–burger.

31 Upper St
Islington, London N1 0PN

Tel: 020-7359 9117

Open: *Mon–Sat* 9.00–18.00
Sun 11.00–17.00

Tube: Angel

This shop has a small take–away section with sandwiches and pastries and also a chiller cabinet with vegan ice–cream, vegan yogurt, veggie sausages and fishless fishcakes.

Barnsbury Health Foods

Health food shop

285 Caledonian Road
London N1

Tel: 020-7607 7344

Open: *Mon–Sat* 8.30–18.30
Sun closed

Tube: King's Cross

Wholefoods, cruelty–free cosmetics, vegan supplements. Take–away with vegan pasties and various veggie snacks. Vegan ice–cream and yoghurts.

Chapel Market

Yer actual London street market

31 Upper St
Islington, London N1 0PN

Tel: 020-7359 9117

Open: *Tue–Wed, Fri–Sat*
9.00–18.00
Thu, Sun 09.00–16.00

Tube: Angel

Full on London street market with all sorts of bargains for the home, fruit and veg, clothing, and great cheap veggie eateries nearby.

CTV

Asian vegan buffet restaurant

22 Golders Green Rd
Golders Green
London NW11 8LL

Tel: 020-7794 0848

Open: *Every day* 12.00-22.00

Tube: Golders Green

Mouthwatering eat-as-much-as-you-like buffet for £5.00, or £6.00 after 5.30pm and on Sunday. You can fill up on goodies such as chow mein, crispy aubergine, spring rolls, Singapore noodles, Thai curry rice, sweet and sour won ton, and black beans hot pot.

Take-out box £3 or £4.

Unlimited Jasmine tea £1. Detox, organic green or ginseng tea £1.50. Fresh juices £2.50. Orange or apple juice £1.50. They are unlicensed but you can bring your own for a minimal corkage charge.

Cash only.

Pita

Falafel bar

98 Golders Green Road,
London NW11 8HB,
(corner of Hoop Lane)

Tel: 020-8381 4080

Open: *Every day* 11-23.00
except Frid night
and Sat daytime

Tube: Golders Green

Green herby or yellow spicy falafels with humous £3.25, plus other nice take-aways. A few seats. It's by the railway bridge that goes over the main road, next to Baskin-Robbins.

Taboon Bakery

Vegetarian café & take away

17 Russel Parade
Golders Green Road
Golders Green
London NW11 9NN
Tel: 020-8455-7451

Open: *Sun-Thu* 19.00-midnight
Fri 10.00-15.00
Sat closed
Tube: Golders Green

Kosher bakery with lots of veggie options to choose from. Take-away snacks including hot potato, mushroom or aubergine latkas, pizza and falafel. Some vegan snacks available but advisable to check which ones are parve (dairy free). There is also a small seating area

Holland & Barrett

Health food shop

17 Temple Fortune Parade,
London NW11
Tel: 020-8458 6087

Open: *Mon-Fri* 9.00-18.00,
Sat 9.00-17.30
Sun 10.00-14.00
Tube: Golders Green

Lots of great take away food here, falafels, pasties, pies sandwiches, salads, many vegan. Two trained nutritionists on site so advice always available. They stock vitamins and minerals and they are happy to order anything for you.

Holland & Barrett

Healthfood shop

81 Golders Green Road
London NW11 8EN
Tel: 020-8455 5811

Open: *Mon-Sat* 8.30-18.30
Sun 11.00-17.00
Tube: Golders Green

This store has a freezer section with veggie sausages, burgers and dairy-free ice-cream but no take-away section..

VitaOrganic

Vegan organic Asian and raw food restaurant and juice bar

Open:
Mon–Sun 12–15.00
18–21.00 (last order)

www.vitaorganic.co.uk for menus

279c Finchley Road,
West Hampstead,
London NW3 6ND
Tel: 020–7435 2188
Tube: Finchley Road,
Finchley Road & Frognal BR

100% vegan organic international and raw living foods restaurant with a gorgeous self-serve buffet for £6.90. Lovely oriental atmosphere with Chinese lanterns, bamboo and friendly staff. It is especially ideal for those on a wheat free, food combining, raw or macrobiotic diet. If you thought raw food was about self-denial, just wait till you try their live vegetable grain free noodles, dough free pizza crackers or tortilla with guacamole.

The buffet includes lots of raw vegetables and Malaysian, Thai, Chinese and Japanese dishes such as seaweed soup, teriyaki, Malaysian tempura, Chinese five spice, Thai or Malaysian curry. Starter plate £4.90, main plate £6.90, starter and main £8.90, one visit, no cheating by sharing plates!

A la carte soup of the day £2.50, other raw or cooked soups £3.90. Main portions include some amazing raw food concoctions £7.90, with rice £1, noodles £2. Innovative global dishes such as golden dream stroganoff; black bean sprouts seaweed stew; green pesto steam fried vegetables; orange masala sprouted dal; red pepper steamd moussaka. Dishes not cooked above 100C to maximise nutrient retention. Mock chicken or prawn £2.50. Steamed couscous, brown rice, millet or quinoa £1.60–3.50. Seasonal economic dishes £4.90.

Healthy guilt-free and sugar-free desserts such as fruit crumble, a raw blend of mixed fruit with seed topping.

Juice bar with lots of blended Juices and seed milks £1.80–3.90. Herbal teas.

If you like this you'll probably the Little Earth Cafe (Camden) or Organic13 (North London) which also have lots of organic raw food.

Friendly Falafels

Falafel stall

15-17 South End Rd
Hampstead, London NW3
(In front of House of Mistry
shop)

Open: *Wed-Sat* 19.30-24.00
Sun 13.30-24.00

Tube: Hampstead Heath

Since 1989, falafel stall in front of the House of Mistry health food shop next to Hampstead Heath.

Falafel £3.40, with hummous £3.90. Salad in pitta £2.50, or with hummous too. 6 falafel balls £1.50. Also Whole Earth cola, lemonade, tea, coffee.

Hampstead Health Food

Vegan & veggie health foods
& take-away shop

57 Hampstead High Street
London NW3 1QH

Tel: 020-7435 6418

Open: *Mon-Sat* 10.00-18.00
Sun & bank holiday:
9.00-18.30
Closed: 25-26 Dec

Tube: Hampstead

Health foods and a wide selection of take-away, some organic, with lots of vegan options including cottage pies, veggie sausages, rice and curry, cakes and flapjacks. Organic dried fruit, nuts and seeds. They stock the complete Ecover range and also have green cosmetics.

Holland & Barrett NW3

Health food shop

14 Northways Parade,
Swiss Cottage, London NW3 5EN

Tel: 020-7722 5920

Open: *Mon-Sat* 9.00-17.30
Sun closed

Tube: Swiss Cottage

Usual range of health and wholefoods.

Peppercorn's

Healthfood shop & take-away

193-195 West End Lane,
West Hampstead,
London NW6 1RD

Tel: 020-7328 6874

Open: *Mon-Sat* 9.00-19.30
Sun closed

Tube: West Hampstead

Organic wholefood store selling everything for veggies including tofu and tempeh, every kind of pasta and health food.

Wide selection of take-away

and macrobiotic specialities from around the world, some organic, with lots of vegan options including Mexican bean slices, vegetarian rotis, country pies, vegetarian sushi, spinach filo pastries, tofu parcels, rice rolls, organic hummous, cottage pies, veggie sausages, rice and curry, cakes and flapjacks. Most dishes, snacks and cakes have ingredients displayed and if they're gluten, sugar free or vegan.

Also supplements, vitamins and minerals, plus Ecover cleaning products.

Staff are well trained and have in depth knowledge of what's what.

10% discount for Vegetarian and Vegan Society members, and senior citizens on Wed.

House of Mistry

Health food shop

15-17 South End Rd,
Hampstead, London NW3

Tel: 020-7794 0848

Open: *Mon-Fri* 9.00-18.00
Sat-Sun closed

Tube: Belsize Park or
Hampstead Heath BR

Health food shop owned by Mr Mistry, a renowned vegetarian health food nutritionist who is currently producing organic products such as insect repellent for plants and humans, and won the Indian equivalent of an M.B.E. for his outstanding achievements with neem, an Indian tree from which many products are made. He has a catalogue of products which are available by mail order worldwide. Cosmetics, body products, oils and toiletries, all of which are definitely not tested on animals.

Organic 13

Open:

Mon–Sat 9.00–18.00
Sun 9.00–17.00
(will be opening evenings)
Children welcome, play corner ,
toys, baby changing, high chairs.
MC, Visa. No smoking or alcohol.

13 Brecknock Road
London N7 0BL
Tel: 020-7419 1234
Tube: Tufnell Park, Camden
Town, Kentish Town, Bus 253,
19
www.organic13.com

Gorgeous new 100% organic Soil Association certified cafe, very close to Bumblebee wholefoods. One kitchen is vegan, the other raw vegan, though they have some dairy stuff on the counter for those who want it. They make all food fresh daily, label all ingredients and whether raw, macrobiotic, living food, wheat and gluten free. Raising standards all round, they filter their own water, have a solar powered sound system, and label any itmes that are non-vegan.

10% discount for Vegan and Vegetarian Society, Green Party.

Full English or light break-fasts.

Hot main dishes £6.95 with salads, such as chilli beans with brown rice, falafel, vegiburger, pasta or wok of the day, dish of the day. Soup £2.95–4.95.

Salad bar small £3.95, medium £6.95, large £9.50 with sprouts, greens, lots of vegetable salads, vegan feta, everything clearly

Ciabatta or panini sandwiches £3.95 with your choice of ingredients from Mediterranean vegetables, greens salads, hummus, garlic sauteed mushrooms, seed pate etc.

Freshly juiced juice blends £3.95. Echinacea or spirulina shot £1, wheatgrass £1.50. Sparkling whole earth drinks £1.25.

Teas and herb teas £1.50 for a pot. Coffee, latte, cappucino, hot chocolate £1.50-2.00 and no vegan tax on soya milk.

If you like this you'll probably like the Little Earth Cafe in Primrose Hill (see Camden section).

eco13

Green lifestyles shop

13 Brecknock Road
London N7 0BL

Tel: 020-7419 1234

Open: *Mon–Sat* 12.00–15.00
         Sun   closed

Tube: Bus 253, 19
www.eco13.com
info@eco13.com

In the Organic13 cafe building, this shop sells and promotes eco products and green lifestyles including energy saving, recycled and renewable materials.

Wind up radios and torches, water powered clock. Eco and hemp books. Hemp and organic cotten T-shirts. Natural paints, varnishes and shoe polish. Serious juicers. Recycled notepads, pens and pencil cases. Organic fair trade cotton Gossypium babygrows, blankets and hats, yoga wear. Organic cottom, buds, bio-degradable nappies and nappy sacs. Vegan Condomi condoms. Bio-D household product refills. Essential Care beauty products. Star Child incense and smudging products from Glastonbury. Magazines.

Phoenicia

Mediterranean cafe and food hall

186–188 Kentish Town Road
London NW5 2AE

Tel: 020-020-7267 1267

Open: *Mon–Sat* 09.00–20.00
         Sun   10.00–16.00

Tube: Kentish Town

Great Lebanese cafe and grocery with deli counter. Point to what you want including hummous, baba ghanoush (aubergine) dip, mixed vegetable grill, wraps, panini. Groceries include self-serve olives, fresh roasted nuts, fruit and veg, fresh herbs, Mediterranean breads.

Outside catering from an office lunch to weddings. Free local delivery over £20.

Rani

Vegetarian Gujarati & South Indian

Open:

Mon–Sat 18.30–22.00
Sun 13.00–15.30
then 18.00–22.00

MC, Visa, Amex

7 Long Lane, Finchley,
London N3 2PR
Tel: 020-8349 4386
Tube: Finchley Central

Home-style Gujarati cooking at the top of Long Lane. Rani won the Good Curry Guide Best Veggie Restaurant Award 2001. Vegan friendly as they don't use egg at all and only vegetable ghee.

5 cold and 11 hot Indian starters, 3 soups, and 2 appetisers £3.20–£3.70.

There are 12 main dishes such as bhindi fried ladies fingers (okra) delicately spiced and slow cooked with whole baby potatoes and onions at £5.40; matar gobi cauliflower florets and garden peas slow cooked with fresh spices and chopped coriander into a dry curry £4.60. Some dishes have an African influence such as akhaa ringal, Kenyan aubergine slit and pressed in spices, ground peanuts and fresh coriander and cooked with potato.

Excellent breads – the essential accompaniment to Gujarati food. Don't miss the mithi roti, a sweetened lentil mix with cardamon and saffron, parceled in unleavened dough, roasted in vegetable ghee, sprinkled with poppy seeds.

10 desserts all under £3, but only the fresh fruit salad is vegan.

House wine £1.90 glass, £9.70 bottle. Small Cobra Indian beer £2.50, large £4.40.

If you like this you'll probably enjoy a trip to the many Indian vegetarian restaurants in Wembley.

Queens Wood

Vegetarian café

Open:
Sat–Sun 10.00–18.00
weekends only
close 17.00 winter

42 Muswell Hill Road
Highgate Woods, Highgate
London N10 3JP
Tel: 020-8444-2604
Tube: Highgate

This hideaway veggie café, part of the Cue Environmental Centre in Highgate Wood, was once a woodkeeper's cottage. They aim to use organic ingredients from their garden whenever possible, and the electricity and lighting is supplied by a solar panel. You can eat on the verandah or sit inside.

It's 5 minutes from Highgate underground station in the woods, easy to find, next to a builders' merchant off Muswell Hill Road

Starters and appetisers £3.50 such as carrot and coriander soup with bread, peanut soup with spinach and sweet potato, olive or mushroom paté on toast, spicy Mexican bean paté.

Main dishes with salad £4.90–5.90 vary, but could include pasta bake, chickpea and broccoli curry, falafel with pitta bread, shepherd's pie, hot pot, or tortilla wrap. Some vegan options available.

Desserts include passion cake, banana cake, chocolate tart and apple crumble with custard, but none vegan though they could all so easily be.

Tea £1, cappuccino £1.50, they have soya milk. Juice £1.20. Wine £2.30 a glass, beer £2.30.

The café is available for private hire and very popular for children's parties, with treasure or fairy hunts in the woods followed by lunch. Also available to hire for environmental group meetings or birthday parties for adults. Children and dog friendly, dogs get a bowl of water.

If you like this you'll probably like Cicero's on Clapham Common (South London).

127

Peking Palace

Open:

Mon–Fri 12.00–15.00,
18. 00–23.00
Sat–Sun 18.00–23.00
MC, Visa. No smoking.
Half buffet portions for children.
Catering for private parties.

669 Holloway Road
London N19 5SE
www.thepekingpalace.com
Tel: 020–7281–8989
Tube: Archway, or Holloway Road and then bus
Bring your own wine.

Lovely vegan Asian restaurant with western specials in the centre of North London with London's biggest vegan menu, currently 115 options. They now have Chinese, Vietnamese and Malaysian chefs. The décor is modern, bright and clean with deep reds and ochre yellows and beautiful paintings and flower displays that give the restaurant a lavish feeling.

Take-away buffet with 14 dishes Mon–Fri £3 small, £4 large, or one large plate eat in £4.95. Half portion for children £2.50.

18 appetizers £3.00 to £4.80 like grilled Peking dumpling; vegetarian satay; asparagus tempura; soya drum sticks or capital soya spare ribs. Range of soups from £2.50 like spinach, tofu and soya chicken.

Second course could be crispy aromatic "duck" served with pancakes and hoi sin sauce for £6.50.

The main course menu is divided into soya meat, tofu dishes, and curries. Try the sizzling soya beef steak Peking style which is very filling for £5.00, fried soya fish in black bean sauce with olive £4.80, or Kung Po soya king prawn for £5.00. 7 kinds of tofu dishes such as big braised tofu steak in black pepper sauce on a bed of cabbage £4.40.

Fake fish steaks and even vegan fish and chips with a big plate with two pieces of fake fish with mushy peas and grilled tomatoes £6.80. Also deluxe vegan cheese-burgers.

Desserts include several flavours of vegan ice-cream £3.25. Toffee and banana with ice-cream, or rambutan stuffed with pineapple in lychee syrup.

Non-alcoholic wines and beers. Fresh pressed juices.

Alternative Health Shop

Health food shop

1369 High Road
Whetstone, London N20 9LN

Tel: 020-8445 2675

Open: *Mon–Sat* 9.00-18.30,

Tube: Totteridge and Whetstone
then 15 minute walk

Vegetarian healthfood shop
with some take-away items
like sandwiches, some are
vegan. Also homeopathic
supplies, supplements, body
care, natural remedies.

Bumblebee

Wholefood & macrobiotic shop

30, 32 and 33 Brecknock Road
London N7 6AA

Tel: 020-7607-1936

Open: *Mon–Sat* 9.00-18.30,
Thurs till 19.30

Tube: Kentish Town

Three shops with a massive
selection of wholefoods,
health foods, organic
produce, macrobiotic foods
and a bakery section which
sells organic bread delivered
daily from organic bakers.
Enormous selection of vegan
and organic wines and beers,
probably the biggest in
London.

Takeaway foods and lunches
11.30-15.00 £1.75
standard, £3.20 large,
always at two vegan hot
dishes based around rice,
tofu quesadillas, tofu
pasties, burritos, samosas.

Box scheme for organic fruit
and veg and delivery service
for other produce.

Some exclusive brands such
as Canadian wheat-free
Tinkyada pasta – "the best in
the world." Big range of
south European foods and
olive oils.

B Green Health Food Plus

Health food shop & take away food

104-106 Ballards La.
London N3 2DN

Tel: 020-8343 1002

Open: *Mon–Sat* 9.30-17.30
Sun closed

Wholefood shop with sand-
wiches and pasties take-
away selection with vegan
options and some cakes,
supplements, cruelty-free
toiletries.

Organic Healthfood store

Organic store

756–758 Holloway Rd
London N7 6QA

Tel: 020 7272 8788

Open: *Mon–Fri* 07.00–21.00
Sat 19.00–23.00
Sun closed

Tube: Archway

Great selection of soya products, tofu steaks. Lots of oganic fruit and veg. Massive selection of organic wine, beer and unusual imported low/non alcohol drinks.

Really well stocked. Environmentally friendly organic paint, towels, clothing.

Holland & Barrett

Health food shop

452 Holloway Road,
London N7 6QA

Tel: 020-7607 3933

Open: *Mon–Sat* 9.00–17.30
Sun 11–17.00

Tube: Archway

Health food store. Fresh take-away food delivered on a Monday like veggie pies, pastries and sandwiches. Dairy-free ice-cream.

Jai Krishna

Vegetarian resturant

161 Stroud Green Road
Finsbury Park, London N4 3PZ

Tel: 020-7272 1680

Open: *Mon–Sat* 12–14.00
17.30–23.00
Sun closed

Tube: Finsbury Park

No credit cards. Cash, cheque with card or LV.

Vegetarian South Indian and Gujarati restaurant not far from the 'Gunners' ground.

There is a wide range of veg and vegan starters such as pakoras, katchuri (lentils in puff pastry) for £1.80.

Mains such as dosas, 35 kinds of curry, £4.50. Thalis £6.75. Try the coconut and lemon rice, and they have brown rice. There are lots of special dishes such as pumpkin curry £3.25.

The usual Indian desserts plus mango slice or mango pulp for £1.95.

Very good value and can get busy, so worth booking on Fri or Sat nights. Corkage £1.25 bottle of wine, 30p a bottle or can of beer, and there's an off license opposite.

Just Natural

Organic food shop

304 Park Road
Crouch End
London N8 8LA
Tel: 020-8340 1720

Open: *Mon-Fri* 9.00-19.00,
Sat 10-19.00
Sun 11.00-15.00

Tube: Alexandra Palace BR

Organic food shop, although not veggie. On the hill not far from Alexandra Palace, so good for picnic supplies. Organic foodstuffs including pastas, noodles, breads, fruit and veg. Organic baby foods, homeopathic remedies, veggie and vegan wines. Local box scheme for delivering organic veg.

They do daily changing fresh lunch vegetarian take-always Mon-Fri such as Moroccan stew with dates, couscous and chickpeas, Tuscan salad with bread, Thai coconut & lentil soup, all £3 for small and £3.50 for a large carton. Veggie and sometimes vegan sandwiches, though not every day, such as humus and salad, also veggie samosas. Fresh juices, coffees, they have soya milk.

Haelan Centre

Wholefood shop

41 The Broadway
Crouch End, London N8 8DT
Tel: 020-8340 4258

Open: *Mon-Thur, Sat* 9.00-18.00
Fri 9.00-18.00
Sun 12.00-16.00

Tube: Crouch Hill, Hornsey BR

Large independent wholefood shop located in hip Crouch End just down the hill from Fiction restaurant, with a complementary health clinic upstairs. They celebrated their 30th birthday in October 2001, making this one of the oldest wholefood centres in London. A great place to buy presents or just little cruelty-free luxuries to pamper yourself.

Ground floor is food, including organic fruit & veg, large fridge/ freezer section with several types of vegan cheese, ice-creams and selection of veggie foods. Well stocked fresh take-away food with vegan options, sushi, pancakes, pies and cakes. Herbs, teas, amazing amount of dry wholefoods and pulses and a good selection of seaweeds and oriental sauces.

The second floor is an Aladdin's cave of non-food items which always smells lovely thanks to the fab toiletries. There is a clinic with a counter which is usually staffed for those wanting to make appointments. Great variety of cruelty-free toiletries, oils, perfumes, soaps, lipsticks, moisturisers, and more cruelty-free shampoos than you've ever seen. Many household products, like environmentally friendly cleaning stuff and vegetable wash.

Ital and Vital Takeaway
Caribbean take-away

134 High Road
Seven Sisters, London N15 6JN

Tel: 020-8211 7358

Open: *Mon-Fri* 9.00-21.00,
Sun closed

Tube: Chalk Farm

Vegetarian take-away salads, Small take-away with Caribbean flavour. Some veggie options like pea soup or ackee, pea and tofu stew, and steamed vegetables.

Mahavir Sweet Mart
Vegetarian Indian take-away

127c High Road
East Finchley
London N2 8AJ

Tel: 020-8883-4595

Open: *Tue-Sat* 11.30-20.30
Sun 11.00-18.30

closed 1 hr for lunch 1 or 1.30
closed Mon

Tube: East Finchley

Indian vegetarian take-away only with bhajias, pakoras, garlic potatoes, curries, vegan puris and of course Indian sweets.

Natural Health
Wholefoods

339 Ballard's Lane
London N12 8LJ

Tel: 020-8445 4397

Open: *Mon-Sat* 9.00-17.30

Tube: Woodside Park, or W263 bus

Vegetarian wholefoods including vegan ice-creams, vegan cheeses and take-away vegetarian and vegan pies, sandwiches, samosas, nut cutlets. Gluten-free, vegan, and special diet ranges. Also homeopathic and herbal remedies, and cruelty-free cosmetics. Good quality vitamins, aromatherapy oils, books, tapes, CDs.

Tai Buffet

Chinese vegan restaurant

271 Muswell Hill Broadway,
Muswell Hill,London N10
Tel: 020-8442 0558

Open: *Every day* 12-12.30

Tube: Highgate or East Finchley
then bus

One of the many Chinese vegan eat-as-much-as-you-like buffet popping up all over London, specialising in fake meats and popular with veggies and non-veggies alike.

£5.50 lunch, £6.50 dinner, or £3 or £4 for a take-away box.

Choose from chow mein, rice, sweet and sour veg "pork" balls, soya chicken, fake beef, crispy seaweed, fried aubergine, spring rolls, tofu and many more. Drinks £1.50. Cash only.

Victoria Health Foods

Health food store

99 Muswell Hill Broadway,
Muswell Hill,London N10
Tel: 020-8444-2355

Open: *Mon-Sat:* 9.00-18.00
Sun: 11-18.00

Tube: Finsbury Park, then W7
bus

Great little health food store, with visiting food allergist every 6 weeks. The manageress Vanya is a nutrition consultant and can give advice.

Very well stocked with large fridge freezer section that has 3 varieties of vegan ice-cream. Plenty of choice for chocoholics also as they stock Bouja bouja gourmet vegan chocs amongst their naughty but nice goodies.

Wide range of dry foodstuffs including wheat-free and diabetic sugar-free sections, and some unique pioneering products from overseas such as candida, IBS, weight loss and skincare products.

Also huge range of herbal and homeopathic remedies and cruelty-free toiletries, toothpaste and household products.

GNC

Health foods & take-away

243 The Broadway,
Muswell Hill N10
Tel: 020-8444 7717

Open: *Mon-Sat* 8.30-18.00
Sun 12-17.00

Tube: Finsbury Park, then W7
bus

Not exclusively vegetarian as

some of their supplements contain gelatin but they don't stock meat products. Some fresh take-away food, usually some for vegans. Non-dairy chocolate and vegan ice-cream. Toiletries and household products.

Holland & Barrett
Health food shop

121 Muswell Hill Road,
Muswell Hill, London N10 3HS
Tel: 020-8883-1154
Open: Mon-Sat 9.00-17.30
Sun 11-17.00
Tube: Finsbury Park, then W7 bus

Fresh take-away snacks such as pies and soya sausage rolls, pastries. Also dried foods, seeds, supplements, vegan ice-cream.

The Veggie House
Vegetarian café and take-away in a community arts centre.

Jacksons Lane Community Centre, 269a Archway Road London N6 5AA
Tel: 020-8348 7666
Open: Mon-Sun 10.00-21.00,
Tube: Highgate

Breakfast from 10am till noon, with a "big daddy's special" for £3.95, as well as separate portions of beans on toast, veggie sausage; scones with jam from £1.00.

Menu changes every day, e.g. soup and bread £3; asparagus and mushroom fan £4.60; sweet potato and coconut stew with coucous (vegan) £4.80; pasta with roast bell pepper and rocket £4.75; vegan shepherds pie £4.75.

Lots of salads, small £2.50, large £3.50.

Desserts £2.50, some of which are vegan, include banana cake and carrot cake.

Tea and herbal teas 60p, coffees 50p-£1, cappuccino £1.50, soya milk available.

Jazz on last Sunday of the month from 12-16.00. Great place to take little ones especially when the theatre in the building has a kids' show every Saturday. Special meal deals for kiddies for £2.50.

Dinner nights every sixth Friday with a theme such as African, Oriental. 2 courses £12.95, 3 for £15. Reserve.

Man Chui 111

Chinese omnivorous restaurant

84 Ballards Lane,
Finchley Central N3
Tel: 020-8349 2400
Open: *Mon–Sun* 12–14.30,
18–23.30
Tube: Finchley Central

Chinese restaurant near the tube station with extensive and tasty vegan section on the menu. Apart from the tofu and veggie dishes, there are many fake meat items.

The Ottomans

Turkish omnivorous restaurant

118 Ballards Lane,
Finchley Central N3
Tel: 020-8349 9968
Open: *Sun–Fri* 12.00–22.00
Sat 12.00–22.30
Tube: Finchley Central

This Turkish restaurant has 21 veggie dishes of which 14 are vegan, such as red lentil soup; vegetable stew with onions, courgette, aubergine, potato and green beens served with salad; imam bayildi – stuffed aubergine on a bed of salad and stuffed vine leaves with rice, sultanas, parsley, onion, dill and pine nuts and salad.

The cold starters are all vegetarian and can be eaten separately for £2.25 each or 7 of them as a mezze for £4.95 per person. Sweets are baklava, cooked pears stuffed with pistachio and chocolate sauce etc – check the ingredients if you are vegan.

They also do take away and special lunch menus which include roast vegetable wraps, and the usual humus/falafel sandwich wrap – all served with chips and salad for £3.95.

Finchley Health Food

Healthfood shop

745 High Road, London N12 0BP
Tel: 020-8445 8743
Open: *Mon–Sat* 9.00–18.00
Sun closed
Tube: Finchley Central

Vegetarian take-away salads, sandwiches, pies and pasties, some of which are vegan. They have a fridge freezer section including vegan ice-cream. Some cruelty-free cosmetics, books, natural remedies, confectionery, cakes, biscuits, chocolate, toiletries and cleaning products.

Mia Bella

Italian onmivorous restaurant

60 High Street, High Barnet EN5
Tel: 020-8441 0022
Open: *Mon–Sun* 12.00 till late
Tube: High Barnet

This Italian restaurant is half way up Barnet Hill not far from the tube station, and their menu has many clearly marked vegetarian items, such as avocado & wild mushroom tagliatelli; tortellini al funghi with wild mushrooms in garlic and herb sauce; spaghetti arrabiata with tomato and chilli; good mixed salads – but suprisingly no pizzas! All food is home made and the staff are very sweet and obliging.

It's great for veggies – vegans must check on some of the ingredients. They say if the dishes aren't big enough for you and you are still hungry after you have eaten, they will give you the same dish again – free! (If Shrek and the WWF On Tour walk in then they'll be sorry!) Free live music on certain nights. Formerly called Mia Natalie.

Grittz

Italian onmivorous restaurant

135 High Street,
High Barnet EN5
Tel: 020-8275 9985
Open: *Mon–Sun* 12.00 till late
Tube: High Barnet

The usual Italian food in this new and very popular restarant with a large wood fired oven and 8 veggie pastas such as penne rusticana with mixed char grilled vegetables, or spaghetti napoli with tomato and basil sauce. Pizzas are freshly made and can be without cheese for vegans.

Burnetts

Onmivorous fushion food

192-194 High Street,
High Barnet EN5
Tel: 020 8441 1413
Open: *Mon–Sun* 12.00 till late
Tube: Chalk Farm

All dining permutations are possible in this restaurant: a snack with a glass of wine, a full blown meal, or afternoon tea at any time of day. The chef has a vegetarian partner, so there are quite a few veggie and vegan options, such as spring rolls with spicy sauce and salad, aubergine stack and salad, most soups, and they do a good assortment of cakes and sweets.

Spizzzico

Italian omnivorous restaurant

135 High Street,
High Barnet EN5
Tel: 020-8440 2255
Open: *Mon–Sun* 12.00 till late
Tube: High Barnet

Another Barnet Italian, pizzas and pastas with lots of veggie options.

Rajen's Vegetarian Restaurant

Indian restaurant & take away

195-197 The Broadway
West Hendon, London NW9 6LP
Tel: 020-8203 8522
Open: *Mon–Sun* 11-22.00
Restaurant
Mon–Fri 12-15.00
Sat–Sun 13-22.00
Tube: Hendon BR

Excellent value Indian vegetarian restaurant and takeaway close to the megacrossroads where the M1 meets the North Circular meets the Edgware Road.

Don't miss their speciality eat as much as you like buffet thali £5 12 till 3pm, £6.50 evenings and all weekend. Also an a la carte menu with lots of fast food items like bhel poori, kachori, masala dosa, onion uttapam, idli, spring roll.

Soft drinks only. Free car park at the back. No smoking. Children welcome, can share with parents if under 5, high chairs available. MC, Visa over £10.

Chandni Sweet Mart

Indian vegetarian take-away

141 The Broadway,
West Hendon, London NW9 7DY
Tel: 020-8202 9625
Open: Mon–Sat 9.00-18.00
Sun 9.00-16.00
Tube: Hendon Central

Indian vegetarian take-away offering samosas, bhajias, but mostly sweets such as jelabi, barfi, ladu, some of them vegan as they use vegetable ghee.

Catering parties & weddings.

Holland & Barrett

Health food shop

Unit W16, Shopping Centre,
Brent Cross, London NW4 3FP
(opposite Waitrose)

Tel: 020-8202 8669

Open: *Mon–Fri* 9.00–20.00
        Sat   9.00–19.00

Tube: Brent Cross

Open quite late to accommo-
date Brent Cross shoppers.

Sandwiches, pasties, non-
dairy ice-cream.

---

115 High Street, Barnet

Tel: 020-8449 5654

Open: *Mon–Sat* 9.00–17.30
        Sun   10.00–16.00

Hendon Healthfood Centre

Health food shop

125 Brent Street,
Hendon, London NW4

Tel: 020-8202 9165

Open: *Mon–Fri* 9.00–18.00
        Sat   11.00–13.00
        Sun   closed

Tube: Hendon

Health food shop with a
selection of organic bread,
some take-away items like
sandwiches, samosas.
Vegan ice-cream, cheese,
yoghurt, eccles cake, raisin
crunch and mince pies.
Vitamins, minerals. Body-
care. Natural remedies.

The Greenhouse

Vegetarian café, take away and wholefood store

Unit 63, Market Hall
Wood Green, London N22
Tel: none
Open: *Mon–Sat* 9.30–18.00
Sun 11.00–17.00
Tube: Wood Green

Vegetarian café (90% vegan), snack bar, take–away and wholefood shop inside covered market hall in Wood Green Shopping Centre.

Homemade soup with bread, pate and toast, various sand-wiches £1.20–3.00. Lite bite salads and savouries £1.20–2.50, mains £3.50–4.00 such as sos roll with meat substi-tutes, fishless fishcakes, curries, pasta, pies, flans, pasties, chilli sin carne, stews, bean bakes, burgers, risotto.

Desserts 60p–£1.50 like homemade cakes and crumbles, flapjacks, always a vegan option.

Special diet such as candida, diabetic etc. can be catered for. Separate smoking area. Cheques but no credit cards. Private functions.

Wholefood store has a well stocked with vegan ice-cream, veggie sausages and burgers.

Holland & Barrett

Wholefood shop

129-131 High Street,
Wood Green, London N22 6BB
Tel: 020-8889-4759
Open: *Mon–Sat* 9.00–17.30
Sun 11.00–16.00
Tube: Wood Green

Usual health foods here. This shop has a freezer section with veggie burgers and sausages and sometimes vegan fishcakeser. Prices £2-3.00.

Pure Health

Wholefoods shop

56 Chaseside,
Southgate, London N14 5PA
Tel: 020-8447-8071
Open: *Mon–Sat* 9.00–17.30
Sun closed
Tube: Southgate

Wholefoods, cosmetics and vitamins. Some fresh take-away items, a few things are vegan such as sandwiches, pasties, samosas.

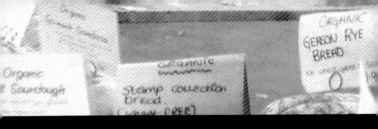

EAST LONDON

GLOBE TOWN

East London *by Claire Ranyard*

I moved to Roman Road in East London a year ago from South London and was immediately struck by the character of the area and the real sense of community. The borough of Tower Hamlets is the most ethnically diverse region of the UK so the influence of lots of different cultures is clearly evident in the types of restaurants, cafes and shops available. I particularly love the wide range of pubs, from the most traditional East End type that almost feels like sitting in your front room to the wonderful organic gastro-pubs around the park such as The Crown.

Victoria Park is a place I really appreciate. It's deceptively big and you can lose yourself and forget for a while that you're in the middle of the city. It even has its own little deer park. The area is also great if you're a cyclist. The canal provides a lovely traffic-free route all the way to Hoxton, Angel or King's Cross to the west and Limehouse and Docklands to the south.

For bargain hunters, **Roma Road Market** (Tue, Thur, Sat) a must. It sells mainly clothe shoes and household good but also has a few good fru and veg stalls that ar extremely cheap. Don't mis the excellent olive stand wher the Turkish owner insists tha you try everything first!

The London Buddhist Centr offers meditation classes an nearby are two Buddhist ru restaurants, a cafe and wholefood store plus the gif shop Evolution.

This area has a real vibrancy t it. It's obviously not the mos prosperous borough of Londo but it's the people and the ric cultural mix which make it suc a wonderful place to live.

142

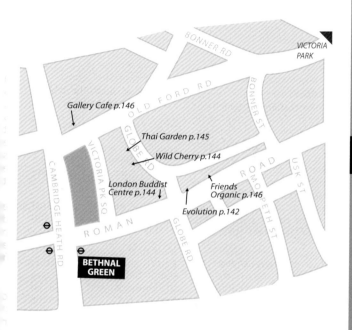

Gallery Cafe p.146

Thai Garden p.145

Wild Cherry p.144

London Buddist Centre p.144 ↓

Friends Organic p.146

Evolution p.142

BETHNAL GREEN

Claire Ranyard is originally from deepest darkest Lincolnshire. She's been interested in animal rights for many years and now spends her days campaigning to end animal experiments by working for the BUAV (British Union for the Abolition of Vivisection). At weekends she can be found bargain hunting in second-hand shops or enjoying a pint of cider in one of east London's many pubs or bars.

Wild Cherry

Vegetarian restaurant

Open:

Mon	11.00-16.00
Tue–Fri	11.00-19.00.
Sat	10-16.00
Sun	closed

Kids welcome   Non smoking
All major credit cards

Veggie & vegan restaurant
241 Globe Road, Bethnal Green
London E2 0JD
Tel: 020-8980 6678
Tube: Bethnal Green
See map on page 143

Cooperatively run vegetarian restaurant, which has a light, spacious feel to it, combined with elegant décor. Sit inside and enjoy the ambience or pop outside to the secluded garden and take a break from the city. They are moving towards as much organic produce as possible whilst retaining affordable prices.

They regularly change the artwork on display, primarily from local artists. Jambala bookshop next door and Evolution gift shop opposite, all linked to the Buddhist centre on the corner. Also a vinyl and secondhand bookshop next door.

Start with soup of the day or a huge range of salads. For mains there is always a vegan option or two, such as aubergine and courgette pilau plus salad £5.25; or veg with spicy & fruity peanut sauce and rice £4.95.

Wide range of homebaked cakes, including vegan, sugar-free and wheat-free, such as banoffee pie £2.85, carrot cake or chocolate brownies.

Saturday all day breakfast includes pancakes and freshly squeezed juices.

Next to the London Buddhist Centre and many meditators pop in before or after classes to enjoy a vast range of herbal teas, home made lemonade and cordials, iced coffee or ginger iced tea-punch, tea, fresh coffee, organic GM-free soya milk. No booze so bring your own and pay £1 corkage.

Outside catering and cakes. Children welcome and they get a lot; 3 highchairs. They also exhibit art.

If you like this you may also like Service Heart Joy in Wimbledon (South London) which also has a spiritual dimension.

Thai Garden

Thai restaurant

Open:

Mon–Fri 12.00–15.00 then
18.00–23.00,
Sat–Sun 18.00–23.00

Kids welcome, high chairs
All major credit cards
Downstairs smoking only

249 Globe Road
Bethnal Green London E2 0JD
Tel: 020-8981 5748
Tube: Bethnal Green

See map on page 143

Thai vegetarian and seafood restaurant where you'll pay a lot less than in the West End. Over 40 vegetarian dishes of which many are vegan. Intimate dining on two floors, the staff are friendly and attentive.

Starters £3.50, or £8.00 for a combination platter for 2 people sharing, such as satay shitake mushrooms in peanut sauce, spring rolls, deep fried vegetable tempura.

4 veggie soups £3.50.

There are 14 vegetable main dishes and another 11 noodle and rice dishes, £4.50. Gang phed ped yang jay was full of flavour, consisting of Thai aubergine, mock duck, pineapple, tomatoes, grapes, bamboo shoots and sweet basil leaves in a red curry with coconut cream. Lard na with fried rice noodles, mushrooms, mixed veg and black bean sauce was also very filling. Other dishes include spicy potato deep fried in chilli sauce, or stir-fried morning glory with garlic and chilli for £5.00. And of course there are Pad Thai fried noodles with peanuts, parsnip, bean sprouts and veg.

Desserts include banana with coconut milk £3.

House wine £2.00 glass, £3.95 half bottle, £7.50 bottle, beer £2.50.

Tea or coffee about £1.50 but no soya milk.

If you like this you may also like the big Thai Square restaurant on Islington High Street. (North London)

Gallery Cafe

Vegetarian café & restaurant

21 Old Ford Road
Bethnal Green London E2 9PL

Tel: 020-8983-3624
Open:
Mon	8.30-15.00
Tue	8.30-15.00
Wed-Fri	8.30-15.00
Sat	10.20-17.00
Sun	closed

Tube: Bethnal Green, then short
walk

Cosmopolitan vegetarian café run as a co-operative by Buddhists with an international menu. Outside umbrella seating in summer on the flower filled south facing terrace.

A different home made soup each day £2.40. Turkish meze starters or filled bagels £1.30-£1.80. Three salads each £1.50. Main course meze £5.30. Hot dishes £4.80 such as Spanish tortilla, casserole or stew, or pasta, sometimes vegan.

Pastries and cakes, sometimes vegan with vegan cream. Juices, tea, coffee and soya milk is always available. Alcohol free, like the people who run the place. Smoking outside only. Cheques and Visa, MC accepted on orders over £5. Children welcome, high chairs.

Friends Organic

Wholefood & organic shop

83 Roman Road, London E2 0GQ
Tel: 020 8980 1843
Open:
Mon,Wed -	9.30-18.00
Thu, Tue	10.30-18.30
Fri	10.00-19.00
Sat	10.00-18.00
Sun	closed

Tube: Bethnal Green

Buddhist wholefood co-op with take-away food and sandwiches, vegan pies and hot and cold snacks such as samosas, which they'll heat up for you. Organic fruit and veg, non-dairy ice-cream and cheeses. Fair trade range and bodycare products. Natural remedies, supplements

The Crown

Organic pub

223 Grove Road
corner of Old Ford Road
Victoria Park, London E3 5SN

Tel: 020 8981 9998

Open: every day 10.30-23.00
Dinner served 18.30-22.30 (Sun 22.00);
Breakfast/lunch Sat-Sun 10.30-16.00, Tue-Fri 12.30-16.00
Tube: Bethnal Green, Stepney Green, Mile End

Only the second certified

organic pub in the world, with progressive policies on renewable energy and they even use bio-degradable cleaning products. The menu changes daily and there are usually at least 2 or 3 vegetarian and vegan options. The desserts are particularly fantastic looking but not necessarily vegan. Organic beer and wine. They've won awards from Time Out, Les Routiers and the Soil Association. Children welcome. Dogs no problem.

Roman Road Market

Street market

Eastern end (Parnell Rd) of Roman Road, E3

Open: *Tue,Thu and Sat*

08.30–17.30

Tube: Mile End

Street market with mainly clothes, shoes & household goods but also has a few good fruit and veg stalls that are extremely cheap.

POGO⚡CAFÉ

DELICIOUS VEGAN FOOD & ALTERNATIVE CULTURE

www.pogocafe.co.uk

76 CLARENCE ROAD • HACKNEY • LONDON E5 8HB • TEL: 020 8533 1214

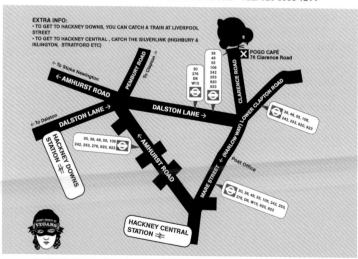

EXTRA INFO:
• TO GET TO HACKNEY DOWNS, YOU CAN CATCH A TRAIN AT LIVERPOOL STREET
• TO GET TO HACKNEY CENTRAL , CATCH THE SILVERLINK (HIGHBURY & ISLINGTON, STRATFORD ETC)

POGO CAFÉ
76 Clarence Road

← To Stoke Newington
← AMHURST ROAD
To Clapton →
PEMBURY ROAD
CLARENCE ROAD

30 · 38 · 48 · 55 · 106 · 242 · 276 · 253 · 920 · 923 · W15

DALSTON LANE →
← DALSTON LANE
← To Dalston

HACKNEY DOWNS STATION

30, 38, 48, 55, 106, 242, 253, 276, 920, 923

← AMHURST ROAD

38, 48, 55, 106, 242, 253, 920, 923

MARE STREET ← (NARLOW WAY) LOWER CLAPTON ROAD
Post Office

HACKNEY CENTRAL STATION

30, 38, 48, 55, 106, 242, 253, 276, D6, W15, 920, 923

JOIN **THE SECRET SOCIETY OF VEGANS**® NOW BUT DON'T TELL ANYONE: IT'S A SECRET.

Pogo Cafe

Vegan cafe-restaurant

Open:

Wed-Sat	12.30-21.00 (last order)
Sun	10.00-21.00
Mon	12.00-18.00
Tue	closed, private parties

Aiming to be open all day 6 days soon, call or check the website.

76a Clarence Road, Hackney
London E5 8HB

Tel: 020-8533 1214

Train: Hackney Central BR
Children welcome, kids' books.
Non smoking. No credit cards.
www.pogocafe.co.uk

New 100% vegan, fair trade, mostly organic, cooperatively run cafe in the premises that used to be Pumpkins veggie cafe. Many of the staff are former Pumpkins fans. An oasis in Hackney with comfy sofas, tables big enough for large groups, children's corner, new wooden floor, spruced up walls with art exhibtions, spot lighting and cool music. International menu. Tasty food with many healthy options.

Sunday breakfast menu features French toast, scrambled tofu and potatoes topped with avocado and sour cream £2.50-3.50.

Lite bites such as quesadillas (wrap with vegan rashers and cheese), burritos, hummous wrap £2.50-3.50.

Starters and snacks such as garlic mushrooms on garlic toast or a bed of salad £2.50; smoked tofu salad with spicy peanut satay sauce £3.

Main courses £5.95 such as curried black-eyed bean ragout with couscous, pitta salad and yoghurt dip; bean burritos with guacamole; cashew nut roast with red cabbage and apple, sweet potato mash and mushroom gravy; Feijoada Brasileira (black beans, vegan sausages, sundried tomato) served with stir-fried cabbage, wholemeal rice and farrofa (stir-fried manioc flour).The best vegan cakes and cheesecake in London, £1-£2, cookies, muffins, some gluten/wheat or sugar free. And vegan ice-cream, yeh.

Shakes, deluxe smoothies with vegan ice-cream, freshly squeezed fruit and veg juices £1.60-2.00. Teas, herbal teas, fair trade Zapatista coffee, soyaccino, latte, soft drinks. Not licensed, offie 5 doors down, £1 corkage.

If you like this you'll probably like Beatroot cafe in Soho (Central) or Cafe Pushkar in Brixton (South) which are also fab for chilling out.

Chandni

Open:
Mon–Sun 17.00–midnight
(last orders 22.30)
Kids welcome
Al major credit cards
Non Smoking

715 High Rd, Leytonstone,
London E11 4RD
Tel: 020-8539 1700
Tube: Leytonstone

Newly refurbished Indian vegetarian restaurant with a few Chinese and African dishes. 85% vegan. They have a bar and outside tables. This is a real find in east London and worth a trip if you'd like a good night out for a lot less than West End prices.

25 starters £1.50–4.50 including vegetable cutlets with potato chips and chutneys, Chinese samosa or spring roll, Pubjabi samosa, dahi wada, Delhi chat, paul bhaji, masala mogo chips, bhel puri, kachori (moong or peas), dal wada, Masala dosa, idli sambar.

17 mains £2.50–5.50 such as vegetable kofta curry, vegetable makhan wala, Punjabi dal fried, chana masala, rajma masala, aloo gobi, Bengan bharta, mixed vegetable curry, vegetable shahi korma, Hakka noodles.

7 kinds of rice from £1.75 to £4.50.

Roti, nan and paratha breads from £1.

Chandni special thali £6.50.

Juices, cold drinks, tea and coffee £1.20. Shakes £2.50–3.00.

Lots of alcohol. Five house wines £6.50–8.00 bottle, £1.70–2.20 glass. Champagne from £17.50 half bottle up to £160 for a bottle of Cristal. (the favourite of MTV hip hop stars) Beers including Cobra from £1.50–1.70 (33cl) to only £2.30 (500cl), a lot less than you'd pay in many places. Aperetifs, spirits and liqueurs £1.80–3.00.

Seating for up to 150.

Party hall with bar.

Outside catering with over 200 items to choose from, all vegetarian, including African dishes.

Spitalfields Market

Organic fruit & veg market

Commercial Street, London E1

Open: *Mon–Fri* lunchtime
Sun 11–15.00

Tube: Liverpool St.

Sunday is the big day with lots of clothes and craft stalls and organic fruit and veg. Look out for Mother Nature's Raw Organic Foods and the Clean Bean Organic Tofu Factory.

There is an east Asian style food market with a wide range of foods where you can eat café style or take-away, and a falafel café.

Soup + Salad

Omnivorous take-away

34 Brushfield Street, London E1
Tel: 020-7377 5756
Fax: 020-7377 5518

Open: *Mon–Fri* 12.00–23.00
Sat closed
Sun 11.00–16.00

Tube: Liverpool Street

Omnivorous take-away and juice bar with lots of veggie food in three sizes near Spitalfields. Soups £1.95, 2.95, 3.95. Salads £2.49, £3.49, £4.49. Smoothies 99p.

Tas Firin

Omnivorous Turkish restaurant

160 Bethnal Green Road
London E2 6DG
(corner Chilton Street)
Tel: 020 7729 6446

Open: *Mon–Sun* 12.00–23.00
Tube: Liverpool Street,
Shoreditch (DLR)

New Turkish place near the top of Brick Lane with several vegetarian mezze dishes. You and a friend can have a few between you with Turkish flat bread (pide) and eat well for £10 or less.

Hookah Lounge

Omnivorous Moroccan style cafe

133 Brick Lane (near the top)
London E1

Tel: 020 7033 9072

Open: *Mon–Sun* 12.00–23.00
Tube: Shoreditch (DLR)

This place is something quite unusual, just south of the bagel shops at the top of Brick Lane, with comfy chairs you can collapse into with a cup of mint tea, or a plate of mezze. The best deal is the £5 vegetarian lunch.

Chawalla

Indian vegetarian restaurant

270 Green Street
Forest Gate, London E7 8LF
Tel: 020-8470 3535
Open: *Every day* 11.00-21.00
Tube: Upton Park

Indian vegetarian restaurant with South Indian, Gujarati and Punjabi food. Really good and vegan friendly. Eat for around £7 a head. Some unusual dishes such as spicy masala potato chips garnished with lime juice, cassava chips with tamarind sauce, lentil and rice pancakes. Desserts include vegan made from gram floue and sugar. No smoking. No alcohol. Visa, MC over £5. Children welcome, high chairs.

Green Street is like a more multicultural Southall or Brick Lane, full of Asian shops run by Sikhs, Muslims, Hindus, Buddhists, even Hare Krishnas, selling henna, incense, clothes and with several restaurants.

Ronak Restaurant

South Indian restaurant & take-away

317 Romford Road
Forest Gate,London E7 9HA
Tel: 020-8519 2110
Open: *Tue-Sun* 12-21.00
      Mon closed
Tube: Stratford, Upton Park, Forest Gate BR

Vegetarian South Indian restaurant and take-away still going strong after over 20 years.

Masala dosa £4, thali with two curries £7.50. Lots of snacks like bhel puri, samosas, kachori. Sunday all day there is an eat-as-much-as-you-want buffet for £4.50 with five kinds of curries.

Desserts include vegan halva and monthar (made fom chickpea flour).

Wine £7.50 bottle, £1.80 glass. Lager £2.80.

Children welcome, high chairs, Disabled friendly. No credit cards. Smoking on one side.

Sakonis Vegetarian

Vegetarian Indian & Chinese

149-153 Green Street
Forest Gate, London E7 8LE
Tel: 020-8472-8887

Open: <u>Winter</u>
Tue-Sat	12.00-21.30
Sun	12.00-21.30

<u>Summer</u>, open half hour later, closed Mon (except bank holiday then closed Tue)

Tube: Stratford, Upton Park, Forest Gate BR

One of three London vegetarian South Indian restaurants that also offer some Chinese dishes.

Most of the menu is same as Wembley (West London) only cheaper. Lunch buffet 12-3pm £5.99 + 10%, so £6.59. Dinner buffet 7-9.30pm (Sat from 6.30pm, Sun from 6pm) £7.99 + 10%. No alcohol sold so BYO. Totally no smoking. MC, Visa.

Tiffin Bites

Indian cafe and take-away

21-22 Jubilee Place
Canary Wharf, London E14 5NY
Tel: 020-7719 0333
Tube: Canary Wharf

Lots of vegetarian dishes. See City (Central) for details.

Applejacks

Health food store & take-away

Unit 28, The Mall
The Stratford Centre, London E15
Tel: 020-8519 5809

Open: | | |
|---|---|
| Mon-Sat | 9.00-18.00 |
| Thu/Fri: | 9.00-18.30 |
| Sun | 10.30-16.30 |

Tube: Stratford

Excellent general healthfood shop. If they don't have it they'll get it within a week.

Most of their take-away range is vegan including the Mexican and blackeye bean wraps, pakoras, rolls, tofu pasties, organic soya cheese pasties, bhajis, nut and mushroom pasties. Carrot cake for afters.

Lots of bodybuilding stuff, natural remedies, supplements includiing Solgar, Viridian and FSC. Books.

Back to Eden

Health food store and take-away

120a Lower Clapton Road
Clapton, London E5 0QR
Tel: 020-8510-9777
Open: Mon-Sat 10-22.00
    Sun 11-21.00

Tube: Chalk Farm

Completely veggie wholefood store with an

Afro-Caribbean flavour. They sell organic herbs, food and spices, fruit and veg such as coconuts, yam. Also some toiletries such as Yaoh hemp shampoo. Good stuff includes vegan hot dogs, tempeh, fishless fishcakes, vegan chicken chunks, spicy bean quarterpounders, soya yoghurt, soya dessert, soya, oat, almond and even quinoa milk. Lots of herb teas. Near Pogo vegan cafe.

Nature's Choice

Health food shop

47 Church Lane
Leytonstone, London E11 1HE
Tel: 020-8539-4196
Open: *Mon-Sat* 9.00-18.30
Sun closed
Tube: Leytonston

Health food shop with organic bread, magazines and books, cosmetics and a small savoury and sweet take-away selection.

Natural remedies, supplements. Chinese medical centre, nutritionist, Reiki, food allergy testing, hypnotherapy, every day by appointment.

Peaches

Health foods & take-away

143 High Street, Wanstead
London E11 2RL
Tel: 020-8530 3617
Open: *Tue-Fri* 9.00-18.00
Sat 9.00-17.30
Sun-Mon closed
Tube: Wanstead

Large range for a small shop with many things you won't find in supermrkets. Apart from the usuals they stock organic English fruit wines and vegan wines. A good range of take-away food and veggie snacks available some days. Lots in the fridge: fake meats, haggis, non-dairy cheese & ice-cream, sprouts on Thursday, Fry's stuff. Tisserand & Amphora aromatherapy and Joss sticks.

Second Nature

Wholefoods & take-away

78 Wood Street, Walthamstow
London E17 3HX
Tel: 020-8520 7995
Open: *Mon-Sat* 8.00-17.30
Sun closed
Tube: Train Wood Street BR

Good selection of organic foods, supplements and sandwiches, pasties and pies and various snacks for veggie and vegans. The focus is on fresh and packaged organic produce and they cater for special diets. They also stock a veggie and cruelty-free range of toiletries, handmade cards, fair-traded gifts, incense, oil burners etc.

Local deliveries and mail order. www.econet.co.uk

Spitalfields Organics

Wholefoods store

103a Commercial Street
Spitalfields, London E1
Tel: 020-7377 8909
Open: *Mon–Sat* 9.30-19.00,
 Sat 10.00-19.00
 Sun 9.00-19.00
Tube: Liverpool Street

Completely vegetarian

wholefood shop with a selection of take-away pies and pasties, plenty of which are vegan. Also a range of organic and non-organic products including toiletries.

Veenus Health Food

Health food shop

141C High Street, Walthamstow
London E17 7DB
Tel: 020-8520-3085
Open: *Mon–Sat* 9.00-18.00
 Sun closed
Tube: Walthamstow

Specialise in teas and vitamins, dry wholefoods. Not exclusively veggie but stock many veggie and vegan foods and organic ranges. Right in the middle of Walthamstow market. And yes, the name is spelt correctly.

Vita Health

Wholefoods Shop

565 Lee Bridge Road, Leyton
London E10 7EQ
Tel: 020-8539 2245
Open: *Mon–Sat* 9.00-18.00
 Sun closed
Tube: Leyton

Usual range of wholefoods and chilled and frozen veggie foods including veggie sausages and burgers, but no fresh take-away. Small toiletries section with cruelty-free shampoos and soaps and a few books. Vitamins and supplements including Solgar.

The Wholemeal Shop

Health food shop

190 Wells Street
London E9 6QT
Tel: 020-8985-1822

Open: *Mon-Sat* 9.00-18.00
      Sun closed

Vegetarian shop with good range that includes organic bread, vegan ice-cream, vitamins, body-building products. Veggie take-away pasties and sandwiches. Bodycare. Homeopathic and herbal remedies.

Holland & Barrett, E1

Health food store

1 Whitechapel High St
London E1 1AA
Tel: 020-7481-3791

Open: *Mon-Fri* 8.00-17.00
      Sat-Sun closed

Tube: Aldgate East

Situated under an office block, this store caters for the surrounding workers. Small take-away selection along with dried foods, supplements and toiletries.

Holland & Barrett, E8

Health food store

Unit 2B, Kingsland Shopping Centre, London E8 2LX
Tel: 020-7923 9113

Open: *Mon-Sat* 9.00-17.30,
      Sun 11.00-16.00

Tube: Dalston Kingland BR

Health food store near Ridley Road maret. Take-away Jamaican, veg and Cornish pasties. Soya cheese and ice-cream soya everything. Frozen pasties, soya sausage rolls, porkless pies.

Holland & Barrett, E15

Health food shop

90 East Mall, Stratford Centre
London E15 1XQ
Tel: 020-8536 0467

Open: *Mon-Sat* 9.00-17.30
      Sun 11.00-17.00

Tube: Stratford

Health food store with soya sausage rolls, pasties, but no sandwiches. But they do have soya ice-cream.

Walthamstow Market

Street market

The entire length of Walthamstow High Street

Open: *Mon–Sat* 9.00–17.00

Tube: Walthamstow Central

The greatest East End street
market with hundreds of
stalls, mostly food. If you
look hard there are incred-
ible bargains like 50p T-
shirts and boxes of mangoes
for a quid. At the Blackhorse
Road (west) end of the
market are some amazing
value grocery stores that are
open outside market hours –
where else could you find
tomatoes for 15p a pound?
Veenus health food store is
on the High Street too.

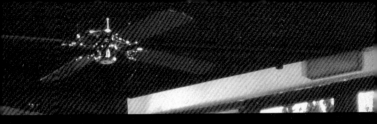

SOUTH LONDON

CLAPHAM & BATTERSEA
South London

Clapham and Battersea are well endowed with green open spaces, a theatre, plenty of shopping and a fine variety of veggie eateries.

Cicero's, in the middle of Clapham Common, is South London's only vegetarian park café. It also makes an unusual private party venue. Battersea Rice (formerly Sayur Mayur, now under new ownership), in Battersea Rise, has a big Chinese vegan menu and is wonderful for take-aways. For partying, head down the road to Wandsworth's Tea Room des Artistes, which ain't no tearoom, but a hip music venue for a great night out with plenty of veggie food. Eco is a regular pizza restaurant that really likes veggies and has vegan calzone.

There are two independent wholefood stores, of which Dandelion has heaps of take-aways. Fresh and Wild wholefoods supermarket has a café and juice bar

Not far from Clapham is Brixton, with its street market and the very popular vegetarian Cafe Pushkar.

Cicero's

Open:

Open daily	10.00–18.00
Summer	10.00–16.00
Winter	Closed Mon

Kids welcome, high chairs
Cheques but no credit cards.
Non Smoking

2 Rookery Road
Clapham Common, Clapham
London SW4 9DD
Tel: 020-7498 0770
Tube: Clapham Common

Vegetarian park café on Clapham Common, near the tube station, in what looks like a converted prefab. International menu and outside seating with some cover for up to 100. A great place to meet your friends and chill out. 50% vegan. Daily changing menu from 12pm.

All day full veggie breakfast £5.50 with huge coffee or tea, £6 with (soya) capuccino.

Starters £3.50 such as sushi with dipping sauce, Taj Mahal soup with bread, Moroccan stuffed aubergine with red pepper sauce.

Main courses £6 such as char grilled tofu with peanut sauce and Singapore rice; aubergine moussaka; pumpkin and chickpea pie curry with rice. Small salad £2.50, medium £3.50, large £5.

Sandwiches, can be made with ciabatta, £2-3.75. Veggieburger special £6 with salad. Also beans or mushrooms on toast from £2.50.

Desserts £2.50-3.00 include vegan chocolate cake, vegan cherry crunch, vegan apple crumble.

Selection of organic teas, organic lemonade, cola, ginger ginseng, Aqua Libra, Amé, elderflower, juices. Organic £1-1.25, others 80p.

12.5% service charge includes corkage if you bring your own booze.

Toys for kids.

Only open in the evening for private bookings of 20 to 25 at £20 per head.

If you like this you'll probably like Hollyhock Cafe in Richmond, Surrey (see South London), another cafe in the middle of a park.

Tea Room des Artistes

Veggie/fish and wine bar

Open:

Tue–Sun:	17.30–01.00.
Sun	15.00–12.30am

Children welcome, no high chairs.
Al major credit cards.
Smoking throughout.

697 Wandsworth Road
(near North St), Battersea
London SW8 3JF

Tel: 020-7652 6526

Tube: Clapham Common

SOUTH

Clapham

Veggie owned restaurant, wine bar and music venue since 1982, in a 16th century barn with original beams and Victorian frontage. A real party place Friday and Saturday. Menu is part vegetarian, part seafood, with many side dishes vegan, and changes regularly so phone ahead to see if it suits as there might be nice veggie dishes on.

Bar snacks and special of the day £7.95 and £9.95. Patatas bravas with spicy tomato sauce £2.95. Thai vegetable samosa with sweet chilli sauce £3.50. Mediterranean mezze of sunblush tomatoes, marinated roast peppers, courgette, artichoke hearts, red onions, olives and toasted pitta bread £5.50. Crispy chunky chips with a choice of dressings £2.95. Leaf salad with balsamic dressing £2.95. Tomato and olive salad £2.50.

Various vegetarian buffets, almost all veggie, for dinner parties of 8 or more people. The Party menu £5 has chunky chips, nachos, crostini, and dips. Indian menu £12 with vegetable korma, pilau rice with mushrooms and spring onions, sweet potato and cauliflower korma, tarka dahl, spiced lemon lentils, garlic naan bread. Oriental menu £12 with red Thai curry, hot red spices with mange tout, babycorn, peppers, carrots and aubergine, lime leaf and coconut rice, veg tempura with sweet dipping sauce, Thai sweet potato samosas, satay fried noodles. Mexican menu £13.50. Mediterranean menu £13.50.

Desserts £3.95 such as apple and cinnamon crumble with dairy-free ice cream.

Extensive drinks menu. House wine glass £2.50, bottle £10.50. House champagne £22.50. Bottled beers £2.60–2.85.

Eco

Omnivorous Pizza place

162 Clapham High Street
Clapham, London SW4

Tel: 020-7978 1108

Open: Mon-Fri 12.00-16.30
        then   18.30-
23.30
Sat   12-23.30
Sun   12-23.00

Tube: Clapham Common

www.ecorestaurants.com

The best pizzas are vegetarian according to the manager, though they weren't sure if the dough base was dairy free, however the vegan calzone is great with pepper and aubergine. This is a pizza place with panache, smartly decorated in light wood and sculptured steel. Allow £6.50-7.50 for a pizza. The garlic bread is done in olive oil not butter. Salads £2.20-3.90, main course £7.80-8.90.

Aubergine and artichoke pizza bread sandwich £6.50. £10.75 for a bottle of wine or £2.75 a glass. Gets pretty crowded so reservations advisable and you are encouraged to leave after an hour and a half, but great fun if you've got the energy.

Fresh & Wild

Organic wholefood supermarket

305-311 Lavender Hill
London SW11 1LN

Tel: 020-7585 1488
Open: Mon-Fri   9.00-20.00
        Sat   9.00-19.30
        Sun   11.00-18.00

Tube: Clapham Junction
        Visa, MC. No smoking.

Organic wholefood supermarket with a huge range of organic produce, fruit and veg, take-away food, remedies and books.

Lots of gourmet, artisan and specialist foods including locally made bread, gluten/wheat free foods. The natural remedies and bodycare section has a qualified herbalist, nutritionist and naturopath.

Café, juice bar and deli with seats and tables. The café has heaps of organic hot and cold food made daily by the in-store chefs, £1.50 per 100g. Salad bar small £2.99, medium £3.25, large £3.99.

For more info on product lines see the Stoke Newington branch. (North London)

Battersea Rice

Oriental Vegetarian restaurant

87 Battersea Rise
London SW11

Tel: none listed
Open: *Mon–Fri* 18.00–23.00
Sat–Sun 17.00–23.00

Tube: Clapham Junction BR

Oriental vegetarian restaurant and take–away. Lots of fake meat and tofu dishes.

Dandelion

Health food shop & veggie take–away

120 Northcote Road, Battersea
London SW11 6QU
Tel: 020–7350 0902
Open: *Mon–Sat* 9.00–18.00
Sun closed

Tube: Clapham South
Clapham Junction BR

Vegan take–away sweet and savoury food a speciality here. Main dishes £2.80 cooked on the premises with at least 20 options including rice dishes, spring rolls, bhajis, samosas, salads, burgers, cutlets. Salads £1–£2. Cakes (occasionally vegan) and vegan apple pie. Organic fruit and veg arrives Tuesday and Thursday. Many other oganic products. Take–away only.

Today's Living

Health food shop

92 Clapham High St.
Clapham, London SW4 7UL
Tel: 020–7622–1772
Open: *Mon–Sat* 9.00–18.30
Sun closed

Tube: Clapham Common

Supplements, oils, frozen foods, remedies and body building products. Sandwiches and pasties, several vegan. They also have freezer counter.

Holland & Barrett

Health food shop

Unit 29, The Arndale,
Wandsworth, London SW18 4DG
Tel: 020–8871 3706
Open: *Mon–Sat* 9.00–17.30
Sun 11–17.00

Tube: Wandsworth BR
Take–away pasties, sos rolls, drinks. Freezer section.

51 St Johns Rd, Clapham
London SW11 1QP
Tel: 020–7228 6071
Open: *Mon–Fri* 08.00–19.00
Sat 09.00–18.00
Sun 11.00–17.00

Train: Clapham Junction BR
This branch has a freezer section and small amount of take–away food.

Cafe Pushkar

Vegetarian café and restaurant

Open:

Mon–Tue 11–17.00
Wed–Sat 11.00–23.00
Sun closed

Children's portions on request, high chairs.
Visa, MC
Non Smoking

424 Coldharbour Lane
Brixton, London SW9
Tel: 020–7738–6161
Tube: Brixton
Directions: Turn left out of Brixton tube, walk past the bus stops and turn left at KFC. It's just past a noodle bar.

Long established vegetarian cafe that started opening as an evening restaurant when they moved out of the covered market a couple of years ago. A lot of people thought they'd closed in summer 2004 but in fact it was just a long holiday. This is a great place to read the paper with a daytime cappuccino and a slice of vegan cake.

Soup, falafel, veg sausages and burgers start at £2.50. Variety of salads, small £2.50 or large £3.95.

The menu of substantial mains, £5 during the day, £6.95 evening, changes every other day, with three specials in the day and five in the evening. Lots of south American influences, north African and far eastern especially, for example Thai green curry; 3 bean tortilla with pumpkin, pepper and guacamole; African sweet potato casserole; Middle Eastern potato stew.

Winter crumbles, cakes and summer fruit salads for £1.00 and upwards.

All cakes cooked on the premises are vegan, such as carrot £1.95, chocolate £2.25. Vegan ice-cream £1.95.

Soya milkshakes £1.95, soya cappuccino £1.30.

Fresh organic juices £2.50.

Wine from £8.95 bottle, £2.50 glass. Organic wine £10.95.

If you're interested in buying the place as a successful going veggie concern, contact Tony.

If you like this you'll probably like the new Pogo Cafe in the premises of what used to be Pumpkins in Hackney. (East London)

Jacaranda Garden

Open:

Mon–Fri 12.00–17.00,
Sat 11.00–18.00
Sun closed

Kids welcome but no high chairs
Cheques but no cards.

11–13 Brixton Station Rd,
Brixton,
London SW9 8PA
Tel: 020–7274 8383
Tube: Brixton

Omnivorous café with 80% vegetarian food offering great value, next to Brixton market and tube station. Very international with an African and West Indian flavour. Quite a large vegan clientele as many dishes are or can be made vegan.

Main courses include vegetarian gumbo, an okra dish £5.90; west African jollof rice served with salads, or Jamaican rice and peas with salad £4.50. Two substantial vegetarian curries with rice £4.20 or pitta £3.80.

Soups are always vegetarian £2.80. Pasta with salad £4.50. Italian focaccia bread is very popular here with hot fillings for £4.20. Also Jamaican patties with salad £3.20. Vegetarian double decker club sandwich £3.20, can be made vegan with avocado.

Desserts include home made cakes £1.50, including vegan sweet bread, and pies such as pecan £2.55.

Fruit juices or filter coffee £1.20, teas and herbal teas 90p–£1.

Bottled beers £2.20, Wine £2.20 glass.

Smoking on the ground floor, non-smoking upstairs. Disabled access.

The owner is interested in selling the freehold as a going concern.

If you like **African food,** check out some of the Indian restaurants in this guide, particularly in Wembley. (West London)

Brixton Wholefoods

Wholefood shop

59 Atlantic Road
Brixton, London SW9
Tel: 020-7737 2210

Open: *Mon-Sat* 9.30-17.30
Mon till 19.00
Fri till 18.00
Sun closed

Tube: Brixton

Great wholefood srore behind Brixton market with take-away pies, pasties, sandwiches, some vegan. Huge range of 'serve yourself' herbs and spices which you weigh so you can have as little or as much as you want. Large range of vegan foods including non-dairy cheese and ice-cream. Organic fruit and veg and good take-away selection. Homeopathic remedies. Bodycare

Brixton Market

Street market

Behind Bixton underground station
Open: *Mon-Sat* 8.00-17.30
not Wed afternoon
Tube: Brixton

Loads of fruit and veg on Electric Avenue and Pope's Road, especially Caribbean stuff like yam and plantain. There are also arcades and a covered market full of shops. The best places to relax are Cafe Pushkar at the south end of the market and Jacaranda Garden Restaurant at the north end.

S.G. Manning

Health food shop

34-36 New Park Rd.
Brixton, London SW2
Tel: 020-8647-4391

Open: *Mon-Fri* 9.00-18.00
Sat 9.15-17.00

Tube: Brixton

Small health food store in a pharmacy towards the south end of Brixton Hill. An astonishing range of wholefoods, non-dairy cheese, organic bread, frozen foods including vegan ice-cream, nut and chocolate spreads. Great for vegans.

Bonnington Cafe

Veggie
wholefood restaurant

Open:
Every day 19.00–23.00
www.bonningtoncafe.co.uk

11 Vauxhall Grove, Vauxhall
London SW8 1TA
Tel: 020-7820 7466
Tube: Vauxhall

Vegetarian wholefood restaurant and garden in a quiet square. Historically a large squatter community thrived here. Nowadays there are as many Mercs as 2CVs. Run on a cooperative basis with a different cook preparing the food each night from their own repertoire, so there is no set menu. The atmosphere is very laid back and it's great value as you can get a three course meal for £10.

Main courses £6. On the day we visited the main courses were roast pepper, red onion and rocket pizza with salad; and spinach and blackeye bean tart with roast potatoes and salad.

There is usually vegan food and Thursday is vegan night.

Visit their website for a map of the exact location behind Vauxhall underground/rail station and for tonight's chef's email and phone number for enquiries such as the availability of vegan food and reservations.

Bring your own alcohol, corkage is free and you can buy booze at the off licence opposite.

Somethimes there is piano music.

Minimum charge of £5 for parties of 8 and over.

If you like this you'll probably like Pogo Cafe in Hackney (East London), which is run in a similar style as a cooperative with different cooks each day.

Kastoori

Open:
Mon-Tue 18.00–22.30
Wed-Sun 12.30–14.30
then 18–22.30
Children's portions, no high chairs
Visa, MC
Smoking throughout

188 Upper Tooting Road
Tooting, London SW17 7EJ
Tel: 020–8767 7027
Tube: Tooting Broadway

There is an east African influence to this vegetarian Indian Gujarati restaurant which doesn't use eggs.

7 starters are marked vegan such as Mogo bhajia, bhel (mix of puffed rice, sev, potato and onions in a sweet and sour sauce), or dahi vada (crispy puris filled with diced potatoes, chickpeas, pani puri sauce and sweet and sour sauce and topped with sev) £1.95 to £4.25.

12 curries, 8 vegan. You could try the Kastoori kofta – mixed vegetable balls, roasted aubergine curry, or a potato curry with the chef's sauce £4.75–5.25.

Thalis 8.50 to £16.75.

Other dishes include dosas, and the range of Kastoori family specials like Kasodi – which is sweetcorn in coconut milk with ground peanut sauce, or kontola curry – made with a crunchy mountain vegetable with garlic sauce.

Lots of side dishes, plus a choice of six desserts – alas only one vegan, the fresh fruit.

House wine £2 glass, £8.95 bottle.

They do outside catering.

If you like Gujarati food you'll find lots more restaurants, some also with East African food, in Wembley. (West London)

Service Heart Joy

Vegetarian café

Open:

Mon-Thu 08.00-17.00
Fri 08.00-21.00
Sat 9-17.00
Sun closed

Kids welcome. Non Smoking.

191-193 Hartfield Road
Wimbledon,
London SW19 3TH
Tel: 020-8542 9912
Tube: Wimbledon

Colourful vegetarian café and take-away, well worth the walk from Wimbledon station to the end of Hartfield Road. Bright yellow exterior, light blue inside with blue tables, yellow chairs and pictures and the peaceful music of Sri Chinmoy which create a tranquil and soothing ambience.

The food is a fusion of modern British and Mediterranean favourites with classic Indian dishes, plus some great vegan cakes.

Cooked breakfasts from beans on toast £2.35 up to brunch £5.45 which includes vegetarian bacon and sausage. Pancakes £3.95, all with maple syrup, include blueberry; banana and walnuts; Balinese style coconut milk, coconut and banana.

Panini or wholemeal sandwiches £2.70-3.40 made before your eyes such as India: with cashewnut butter, mango chutney, green pepper and coriander.

Salads £2.45-5.45. Soup of the day with bread £2.50.

Indian hot dishes £3.95-5.95 such as dhal with rice or potato, Indian platter and special of the day. Veggie burger £3.50. Baked potatoes from £2.45 with baked beans.

Lots of cakes including chocolate, mango, banana and flapjacks.

Smoothies £2.50. Juices, latte, cappuccino, mocha, hot chocolate, teas 80p-£2.40.

They also do catering, much of it vegan.

Previously called Mangoes.

If you like this you may also like the Buddhist run places in Globe Town, East London.

Milan

Open:

Mon	11–21.30
Tue–Thu	10–21.30
Fri–Sat	9–22.00
Sun	9–21.30

158 Upper Tooting Road,
Tooting,
London SW17 7ER

Tel: 020-8767 4347

Tube: Tooting Bec,
Tooting Broadway

Gujarati and South Indian vegetarian restaurant and sweet centre with over half the dishes being vegan (or vegan option) and clearly marked on the menu.

16 starters (13 are vegan) £1.60–2.50 like mogo chips, bhajias, spring rolls, kachori, puris, patties.

They offer 22 main courses (16 vegan), divided into either dosa or curries for £2.50 to £4.95, like veg kofta, mushroom curry, chana bhatura chick pea and potato curry with fried fluffy bread.

Three thalis, £4.95–£7.95. Milan special thali has a vegan option for £7.95 with millet loaf, roast aubergine, moong, rice and papadum. All the usual parathas, nan, dahl, pickles.

8 desserts £1.25–£2.00, two of which are vegan.

Juices like fresh passion and mango from £2.25. House wine £6.50 bottle, £2.00 glass.

Catering for weddings and parties.

If you like this you'll probably like Shahee Bhelpoori down in Norbury (South London) or the many Indian restaurants in Wembley (West London).

Shahee Bhelpoori

Open:

Open every day   12.00–14.30
inc bank holidays   18–23.00,
Sun lunch   12.00–15.00

Children's menu, high chairs
Smoking section

1547 London Road
Norbury,
London SW16 4AD
(opposite Norbury BR Station)

Tel: 020-8679 6275
Train: Norbury BR

Indian vegetarian restaurant with 100 dishes, many of them vegan and virtually anything can be made vegan for you. All dishes marked vegetarian, vegan or can be prepared as eiher.

13 hot and cold starters £1.85–3.05 such as vegetable kebab. 20 side orders from £2.25 include vegetable kofta at £2.95.

Main courses from £2.95 include 8 dosas from £2.95–4.75, 8 thalis £4.50–6.95.

14 desserts £1.65–2.25 include vegan ice cream. An Indian restaurant that recognises vegans don't just eat main courses, which might help explain their popularity with local vegans. And who says you need to be vegan to eat vegan dessert? Do you have to be Indian to eat curry?

Exotic Sunday buffet lunches only £3.95, eat as much as you like. Children under 6 half price.

Children's menu £3.50 with mild masala dosa or French fries with veggieburger and salad, followed by ice-cream on request, can be vegan.

Beer £1.85 pint, wine £6.50 bottle or £1.60 glass. Tea 60p, coffee 90p, soya milk available.

10% discount to Vegetarian or Vegan Society members. Visa, MC. If you present this book you also get 10% discount.

Croydon Vegans meet here, see local contacts, and the local MP comes here for bhel poori.

On the A23 Brighton to London road, so handy on you way back from a trip to the seaside.

If you like this you'll probably like the Indian vegetarian restaurants Kastoori and Milan in Tooting (also south London).

Pepperton UK

Vegetarian
Vegan restaurant

Open:

Tue–Sat 10–22.00
Sun 12–20.00

Licensed

Therapy rooms upstairs

25 Selhurst Rd
London SE25 5PT
(opposite the Selhurst Arms)

Tel: 020-8683 4462

Tube: Selhurst BR,
buses 75, 157

Licensed vegetarian/vegan restaurant and contemporary art gallery open since August 2003. The red front makes it unmissable. A favourite of Croydon Vegans who tell us the food is delicious and most artistically presented, looking more attractive even than some of the paintings and delightful photographs. There are two upstairs rooms for the gallery, and the beautiful staircase was made by the owner from a fallen fruit tree from France. The owner–manager has a huge smile. Vegan and wheat–free items are marked on the menu and you can call ahead with any special requests.

Starters £3.50-3.99 include mung bean pakoras on a bed of fresh salad with a twist of lemon; crudites with hummus. Salads £2.50-4.50 such as mixed with roasted sunflower and pumpkin seeds. Soup of the day with home baked olive bread £4.50.

Main courses are no more than £6.50 such as almond and vegetable fried rice with spinach dhal; wild rice with vegetable curry. Jacket potato with beans £2.50, with selection of cooked toppings £5.50.

Home baked cakes £2.50 such as fruit and nut, vegan muffins 70p. Various desserts such as crumble, not necessarily vegan, but they have vegan ice-cream £2.25.

Teas and herb teas 60p, all kinds of coffees £1-1.80. Mineral water 70p for a glass. Juices 70p-£1. House wine £9.50 bottle, £2.20 glass. Fruit and organic wines £11.50. Alcohol free elderflower wine £6. Organic vodka or gin 25ml £3.50. Organic beers £2-£3.

If you like to look at art with your food, you'll probably like Pogo Cafe or Wild Cherry in East London.

173

Wholemeal Café

Wholefood vegetarian restaurant

1 Shrubbery Road, Streatham
London SW16 2AS

Tel: 020-8769 2423

Open: *Every day* 12.00–22.00
closed on all bank
holidays

Tube: Streatham BR, Streatham
Hill BR

MC, Visa. No Smoking.
Child portions, one high chair.

Wholefood veggie restaurant
with Thai, Indian, Mediterranean and world cuisine.
Large vegan selection.
Typical dishes include garlic
mushrooms with pitta £3.25;
guacamole and warm pitta
£3.25, or soup of the day
£2.50, usually vegan.

Main dishes £2.5–6.50
include homity pie, hot bake
of the day, casserole of the
day, red Thai curry, spinach
and mushroom crumble.

Wholemeal Cafe, Streatham

Desserts £2.50 such as
banoffee pie or wholemeal
fruit crumble with vegan
custard. Soft drinks like Aqua
Libra and organic lemonade.
Teas and coffees. House
wine £3.20 glass, £13.50
bottle. Organic wines, beers,
ciders, ales.

Pili Pili

Indian vegetarian restaurant

26 Embassy Court
Welling, Kent DA16 1TH

Tel: 020-8303 7636

Open: *Tue–Sun*
12–15.00, 18–22.00
Fri–Sat till 23.00;
Mon closed
(except bank holidays)

New vegetarian Indian
restaurant, with some
Chinese food, midway
between Greenwich and
Dartford. Much of the food is
vegan and they can make
non-vegan items with soya
milk on request.

Over 30 bites £1.95–4.50
include uttapam lentil pizza,
dosas, dhokla rice and lentil
pancake, lentil doughnuts,
pani puri, bhel puri, chilli
corn on the cob, potato
fritters, idli, samosas, sev
puri, spring rolls. Main
specials inclide potato curry
with daal bhajia £4.50,

mushroom pitta pocket £5.50, vegetable sizzler £7.50. Indo-Chinese soups and dishes such as Hakka o Szechuan noodles with veg £3.95, sweet and sour veg £4.50.

Desserts £1.95-3.75 include carrot halwa, lychees.

Tea, hot chocolate, cappuccino £1.50. Sodas £1. Seasonal fresh juices £2.95.

Domali

International café bar restaurant

38 Westow Street
Crystal Palace, London SE19 3AH
Tel: 020-8768-0096

Open: *Mon-Tue* 9.30-18.00
Wed-Sun 9.30-23.00

Train: Crystal Palace BR,
Gypsy Hill BR
Child portions.
www.domali.co.uk

Café with a big global menu, 90% veggie and plenty for vegans.

Veggie breakfast served until 6pm, includes muesli, veggie bacon and sausages £1.90-5.90. For lunch they have vegan soup £2.90. Midweek specials include wild mushroom paté with farmhouse bread, olive oil and mixed leaf garnish £3.90; Tuscan bean and veg casserole served with char-

grilled farmhouse bread £6.90; pasta of the day £6.90;layered sweet potato bake with salad £6.90.

Toasties £3.90 include veggie sausage with mustard and tomato, or veggie salami with roasted pepper. Vegan sandwiches include houmous and carrot, veggie BLT £2.50-2.90.Coffee and juice bar with soya smoothies, double juices £2.20, singles £1.60. Add a shot of St. John's Wort, echinacea, gurarana or milk thistle for 40p. Large drinks list includes house cocktails and wines. Happy hour every evening 6-8pm, half price cocktails.

Local artists' work is exhibited and it's for sale. Sunday night DJ.

Mantanah Thai Cuisine

Thai restaurant

2 Orton Buildings,
Portland Road, South Norwood, London SE25 4UD
Tel: 020-8771 1148

Open: *Tue-Sun* 18.30-23.00
Mon closed

Train: Norwood Junction BR
(Thameslink)
www.mantanah.co.uk for recipes and prices with veggie ones at /veg1.htm to veg3.htm

Thai restaurant in deepest south London towards Croydon. Like many Thai restaurants, this one has as many veggie dishes as some vegetarian restaurants.

Starters from £3.50–4.70 such as spring roll, golden veg with pepper, sweet potato and plum sauce, deep fried pumpkin, tom yum soup, spicy mushrooms with coconut milk.

Main dishes include the Thai classics of red and green curry £5.25 plus steamed, coconut or sticky rice £1.65–3.50. Mixed veg £3.75–4.00. You could also try the exotic spicy banana flower with oyster mushrooms and steamed sweet potato. Choice of salads. Licensed for wine and beer including Thai Singha beer.

Wagamama Putney

Japanese omnivorous restaurant

50–54 High Street, Putney, London SW15 1SQ
Tel: 0208 785 3636
Open: *Mon–Sat* 12.00–23.00
Sun 12.30–22.00
Tube: Putney Bridge
www.wagamama.com

The newest Wagamama, opened October 2004. See Bloomsbury, Central London, for menu, or their website.

Ambala Sweets

Indian vegetarian take-away

48 Upper Tooting Road, London SW17 7PD
Tel: 020-8767 1747
Open: *Mon–Sun* 10.00–20.00
Tube: Tooting Bec
www.ambalaoods.com

Vegetarian take-away with Indian sweets, samosas, pakoras, but not vegan.

Baldwin's Health Food

Health Food Shop

171 Walworth Road
Walworth, London SE17 1RW
Tel: 020-77014892
Open: *Mon–Sat* 9–17.30,
Sun closed
Tube: Chalk Farm

Hot and cold take-away selection of sweet and savoury goodies, also supplements and green toiletries. They no longer stock organic fruit and veg. Informative noticeboard.

Balham Wholefood

Health food shop

8 Bedford Hill, Balham
London SW12 9RG
Tel: 020-8673-4842
Open: Mon–Sat   9.30–18.00
Tue–Thur –19.00
closed for lunch 13.30–
14.30
Tube: Balham BR

Health food shop with a large
range of dried fruit, seeds,
pulses etc, both organic and
non-organic, and books.
Swedish Glace vegan ice-
cream.

GNC Putney

Health food shop

151 Putney High Street
Putney, London SW15 1SU
Tel: 020-8788-0944
Open: *Mon–Sat* 8.30–18.30
Sun   9.00–18.30
Train: Putney BR

Freezer products like veggie
sausages and burgers and
veggie mince.

Herbs, vegan chocolate, but
no fresh take-aways at this
branch. Large range of
vitamins and minerals, some
veggie and vegan.

GNC Wimbledon

Vegetarian & vega n take away

Centre Court Shopping Centre
Queens Road, Wimbledon,
London SW19
Tel: 020-8947 3583
Open: *Mon–Fri* 9.30–19.00
Thur   –20.00
Sat   9.00–18.00
Sun   11–17.00
Tube: Wimbledon

No take-away items available
here but they have a freezer
section.

Greenlands Health

Health food shop

Unit 3a, Greenwich Craft Market
Greenwich, London SE10 9HZ
Tel: 020-8293 9176
Open: *Mon–Sun* 9.30–18.30
Tube: Greenwich

Health food store with all
vegetarian take-away pies,
pasties, snacks £1–3.75.
Sandwiches from £1.79,
salads £1.79. Also some
cakes and health drinks.

Health Zone Ltd

Health food shop

30 Wimbledon Hill Road
Wimbledon, London SW19 7PA

Tel: 020-8944-1133
Open: *Mon–Fri* 9.30–19.00,
      Sat   9.30–18.00
      Sun   11–17.00
Tube: Wimbledon

Much more than your average health food shop, with a vegan manager and a complementary therapy clinic attached.

They stock a wide range of veggie and vegan foods, many organic, supplements and organic body-care products.

Also a few veggie/vegan sandwiches, falafel in pitta, pasties, pies, salads such as couscous, from £2 upwards and a gluten-free range. Vegan ice-cream.

Yoga and pilates equipment. Wide selection of books on health, magazines, CD's.

Health Food Centre

Health food shop

156 Balham High Road, Balham
London SW12 9BN

Tel: 020 7586 8012
Open: *Mon–Sat* 8.30–18.30
      Sun   9.00–18.30
Tube: Balham

Health foods but no fresh take-away. Vitamins, homeopathic remedies, aromatherapy oils.

Nature's Way

Health food shop

252 Streatham High Road,
Streatham, London SW16 1HS

Tel: 020-8769-0065
Open: *Mon–Sat* 9.30–18.30,
      Sun   closed
Train: Streatham BR

There are 2 floors to this vegan owned health food shop. They have a very large range of foodstuffs on the lower floor, while on the upper floor are supplements, remedies, oils, green products, stationery and cruelty-free cosmetics. People come from a long way to shop here.

There's plenty for vegans including the whole Plamil

range. All the take-aways are veggie or vegan and include carrot cutlets and eccles cakes.

Indian head and back massage. Allergy testing. 5% discount for Vegetarian and Vegan Society members.

Provender Wholefoods

Wholefood store and vegetarian cafe

103 Dartmouth Road, Forest Hill
London SE23 3HT

Tel: 020-8699-4046
Open: *Mon-Sat* 8.30-18.30
Sun 10.30-16.30

Train: Forest Hill BR

Friendly wholefood store and café with vegetable bake and pasties, salads and rolls to take away.

They make their own organic bread. Organic fruit and veg arrives Thursdays.

Wholefoods for sale and some books.

New branch opening in East Dulwich in February 2005 at 51 North Cross Road, SE22.

Sheel Pharmacy

Health food shop & take-away

312-314 Lewisham Road
Lewisham, London SE14

Tel: 020-8297-1551
Open: *Mon-Fri* 9.00-19.00
Sat 9.00-18.00
Sun closed

Not just a pharmacy, they have savoury take-aways and cakes. Wide range of vegan foods and cosmetics.

10% discounts for Vegetarian and Vegan Society members. Chiropodist and osteopath on the same site.

Vitality Health Foods

Health food shop

Savacentre, 1 Merton High Street
London SW19 1DD

Tel: 020-8544-9433
Open: *Mon,Tue-Sat* 9.00-20.00
Wed 10-18.00
Thu 9-20.30
Fri 9-19.30
Sun: 11.00-16.30

Tube:

Small health food sore. No fresh take-away, but plenty of other dried goods and health foods available

Well Bean

Healthfood store

9 Old Dover Road, London SE3
Tel: 020-8858 6854
Open: *Mon-Fri*   9.00-18.00
           Sat-Sun   9-17.00

Vegan manager here so plenty of vegan grub. Gluten-free range. Vegan ice-cream. 10% Vegetarian & Vegan Society discount with card.

Well Being Foods

Wholefoods and organic shop

19 Sydenham Road
London SE26 5EX

Tel: 020-8659-2003

Open: *Mon-Sat* 9.00-18.00
         Sun   closed

Complete selection of whole foods and organic fruit and veg, plus take-away pies, pasties, salads, fresh breads and some cakes, and a good freezer selection. Body care & household products range.

Holland & Barrett

Vegetarian & vega n take away

31 Tranquil Vale,
Blackheath, London SE3

Tel: 020-8318 0448

Open: *Mon-Sat* 9.00-18.00,
         Sun   11-16.00

Vegetarian sausage rolls, pasties. Swedish Glace vegan ice-cream.

81 Powis Street, Woolwich
London SE18 8LQ

Tel: 020-8316 5490

Open: *Mon-Sat* 9.00-17.30,
         Sun   10-16.00

This branch has a freezer with vegan ice-cream.

68 The Broadway, Wimbledon
London SW19 1RQ

Tel: 020-8542 7486

Open: *Mon-Sat:* 9.00-17.30,
          Sun   closed

This branch of Holland and Barret has a freezer section and weekly deliveries of fresh take-away food.

3 Mitcham Rd, Tooting
London SW17 9PA
Tel: 020-8767 8552
Open: *Mon-Sat:* 9.00-17.30,
         Sun   10-16.00

Freezer section for those important purchases of vegan ice-cream. They also stock some fresh take-away item like pasties but not sandwiches.

Unit 19, The Aylesham Centre
Rye Lane, Peckham,
London SE15 5EW

Tel: 020-7639 3354
Open: *Mon-Sat:* 9.00-17.30,
Sun 11-16.00

Health food shop with lots of veggie snack food.

---

137 High St, Putney
London SW15 1SU

Tel: 020-8785 7018
Open: Mon-Sat: 9.00-17.30
Sun: 11.00-16.00

This branch has some fresh take-away and also a freezer section.

---

198 Eltham High St, Eltham
London SE9 1TS

Tel: 020-8859 7075
Open: *Mon-Sat:* 9.00-17.30
Sun closed

Health foods and wholefoods here but no freeezer or take-aways, though plenty of snacks.

110 Streatham High Rd.,
Norbury, London SW16 1BW

Tel: 020-8769 1418
Open: *Mon-Sat* 9.00-17.30
Sun closed

Usual range of health foods but no take-away.

---

67 Riverdale Court, Lewisham
London SE13 7ER

Tel: 020-8297 9559

Open: *Mon-Sat:* 9.00-17.30
Sun: 11.00-17.00

They have a freezer section here with vegan ice-cream.

Unit 6, Surrey Quays Shopping
Ctr, Redriff Road, Surrey Quays
London SE16 1LL

Tel: 020-7231 1043

Open: *Mon-Thu* 9.30-18.00
Fri until 20.00
Sat 9-18.00
Sun 11.00-17.00

Regular health food shop. Some veggie sos rolls, pasties, porkless pies.

---

33 Winslade Way, Catford
London SE6 4JU

Tel: 020-8690-3903
Open: *Mon-Sat:* 9.00-17.30
Sun closed

This branch has sos rolls, pasties, porkless pies, non-dairy ice-cream.

Riverside Vegetaria

International vegetarian restaurant

Open:

Every day 12.00–23.00
Sun till 22.30
Kids welcome, 5 high chairs
MC, Visa. Non smoking.
Gluten and wheat free no problem.

Menus at www.rsveg.plus.com

64 High Street,
Kingston-upon Thames, Surrey
Tel: 020-8546 7992
Tube: Kingston BR
Booking advised a week ahead
for weekends and outside.

Superb riverside vegetarian restaurant with large windows that open out over the Thames. Idyllic in summer but well worth the trip at any time of year. In warm weather you can eat under the sky in the outdoor area on the towpath beside the river. 70% vegan with awesome desserts.

Starters £4.50–£5.50 like potato balls with chilli sauce, sweet potato soup, garlic mushrooms, and falafel, veg bowl with coriander sauce, nutty parsnip soup, turnip and chestnut soup.

Main dishes £6.50–£8.50 include masala dosa; string hopper biriyani with fine noodles; tofu marinated in teriyaki sauce, mushroom and lentil bake; all served with veg, salad and/or rice.

A truly great vegetarian restaurant is memorable for its desserts and vegans especially will never forget

Riverside Vegetaria after scoffing some of the vegan desserts like chocolate cake or baked figs with orange and brandy. They even have soya custard. From £3.50.

Lots of soft drinks, liquor, organic beer and even champagne from £28.95. Organic wines and Disos vegan red and white.

10% discount for Vegetarian and Vegan Society members and 20% for clever people presenting this book! Take-away including frozen soup by the litre. Outside catering. Vegetarian Society best restaurant 2002.

Veggie One

Vegetarian
Chinese restaurant

Open:

Tue–Sun 18.00–23.00
Mon closed

Children welcome, no high chairs. Smoking allowed, but they do ask you to consider others and most choose to go outside.

322 Limpsfield Road, Sanderstead, South Croydon, Surrey CR2 9BX
Tel: 020-8651-1233
Tube: Sanderstead train
Cheques or cash, no cards.

Vegetarian Chinese restaurant and take-away, GM free and completely organic. All their dishes are vegan except the egg fried rice. Evening meal £10–15 per person.

For starters try crispy aromatic duck, tempura vegetables, crispy fruit roll in rice paper, deep fried tofu Thai style or dim-sum at £1.80–£6.00.

Mains £2.00–£5.50 include aubergine and bean casserole, vegan pork, vegan fish, abalone mushrooms with sesame.

8 desserts £2.50–4.50 such as toffee apple, toffee banana, mango pancake, fresh fruit, fruit cocktail, lychees, banana or pineapple fritter. Swedish Glace vegan ice-cream £3.50.

Juices £1.50. Mineral water big bottle £3.50. They have soya milk.

House wine £10 bottle, £2.70 glass. Organic wines.

Non alcoholic wine £5.50 or £6 per bottle. Non-alcoholic beer £1.50 or £2.

They have a wholesale vegetarian frozen food business called Vegetarian Paradise, with some items on sale in the restaurant.

Croydon and Sutton Vegans sometimes meet here.

If you love Chinese vegan food then you'll probably also like Peking Palace in North London.

Tide Tables

Open:

Open every day, daylight hours, phone ahead as they close if weather is bad.

Child friendly, high chairs
Smoking outside

2 The Archways,
Richmond Bridge,
Richmond, Surrey TW9 1TH
Tel: 020-8948-8285
Train: Richmond BR
Cash or cheque, no cards.

Vegetarian café under the arch of a bridge near the town centre, with beautiful views of the Thames, a riverside terrace and outside seating in summer, though people sit ouside year round when it's sunny for the view.

All food is GM free and menu items are clearly marked up for gluten-free, organic and vegan.

Child and dog friendly, a nice place to meet friends for lunch.

The breakfast menu offers organic muesli, toasted organic muffin with jam, panini (can be vegan pesto), almond croissants or pain chocolat from £1.35 to £2.90. They have soya milk.

For lunch and tea there's vegan soup, spinach pastie with salad, stuffed focaccia, vegan shepherdess pie with salad, falafel with hummous and salad, jacket potatoes, from £2.20 to £5.40. Also samosas and bhajias.

Handmade cakes, including vegan almond twists, £2.30.

Hot and cold drinks and free corkage. Juices, freshly squeezed organge juice £2.50 for half pint. Cappuccino £2.15 big mug, £1.50 smaller one, soya milk no problem.

They also sell some second-hand books for charity, £1 each or 3 for £2.

If you like this you'll probably also like The Green Cafe and Hollyhock Cafe nearby.

Hollyhock Café

Vegetarian cafe

Petersham Road, Richmond,
Surrey TW10 6UX

Tel: 020-8948 6555
Open: Open from Easter to
Autumn half term, every day,
daylight hours. Closed in Winter.

Child friendly, high chairs.

New vegetarian café, linked
to Tide Tables, in the middle
of a park overlooking the
Thames, with really lovely
views. Very child friendly,
parents sit on the verandah
while kids play on the grass.

Lots of juices and smoothies,
(soya) cappuccino, salads
and baked dishes. They do
veggie breakfasts.

The Green Cafe

Vegetarian café and juice bar

29 The Green, Richmond,
Surrey TW9 1LX.

Tel: 020-8332 7654

Open: *Mon–Sun* 9-18.00

Tube: Richmond BR
Smoking outside only. No cards.
Very child friendly but no high
chairs here as less seating.

Another new vegetarian café,
also similar to Tide Tables,
on picturesque, historic

Richmond Green tucked
behind the main high street,
with outside seating. This
one is more of a specialist
juice bar. Smoothies £3,
fresh fruit and veg juices
£2.50, wheatgrass available.
Always have soya milk. Also
salads, stuffed pitta, soups.

Santok Maa's

Indian vegetarian restaurant

848 London Road,
Thornton Heath, Surrey CR7 7PA

Tel: 020-8665-0626

Open: *Thu-Tue* 12.00-22.00
      Wed closed

Train: Thornton Heath BR,
      Norbury BR

Children welcome, high chairs.
Visa, MC, Amex

North and South Indian
dining and take-away, with
some spicy Chinese dishes
like stir-fries. Nearly 100
dishes. Starters average
£2.95, main courses £3.95,
rice £1.75. Desserts from
£1.50 and they now have
vegan ice-cream. Bring your
own wine, £1 per person
corkage. Special offer on
Monday, all food half price
excluding dessert and take-
away. Outside catering for
weddings and parties.
Eggless cakes.

Swad

Indian Gujarati vegetarian restaurant

850 London Rd, Thornton Heath,
Surrey, CR7 7PA
Tel: 020-8683 3344
Open: *Mon–Fri* 9.00–21.00
       Sat–Sun 10–22.00

Buffet £5–6 12–15.00
starting Jan 2005. Wine £8–
10. Children welcome, high
chair. No smoking. MC, Visa.
Outside catering up to 2,000
people.

Surrey SOUTH

Wagamama Kingston

Omnivorous Japanese restaurant

16–18 High Street
Kingston-upon-Thames
Surrey KT1 1EY
Tel: 020-8546 1117
Open: *Mon–Sat* 12.00–23.00
     Sun 12.30–22.00

Train: Kingston BR

---

3 Hill Street, Richmond
Surrey TW9 1SX 1EY
Tel: 020-8948 2224
Open: *Mon–Sat* 12.00–23.00
     Sun 12.30–22.00

Train: Richmond BR

Omnivorous fast food
Japanese noodle bar with
veggie dishes. See Bloomsbury branch for details.

Food For Thought

Wholefood shop

38 Market Place, Kingston
Surrey KT1 1JQ
Tel: 020-8546-7806
Open: *Mon–Sat* 9.00–17.30
     Sun closed

Train: Kingston

Wholefood shop with
supplements, aromatherapy,
skin-care ranges, and homeopathic remedies.

Oliver's Wholefood

Wholefoods shop

5 Station Approach, Kew
Gardens, Richmond TW9 3QB
Tel: 020-8948 3990
Open: *Mon–Sat* 9.00–19.00
     Sun 10.00–19.00
Tube: Kew Gardens

Wholefood shop with a wide
selection of produce, not all
of it veggie. Good location
next to the tube station and
handy for picking up
something to nibble while
you visit Kew Gardens.

Veggie and vegan take-away
snacks include sandwiches,
pastries, salads, seaweed
rice and wraps. They sell
vegan wines as well as
organic fruit and veg.

The store has a trained nutritionist and beauty therapist on site for advice and there are regular lectures in-store on topics like living food and digestive health.

Holland & Barrett

Health food shop

Unit 44, Ashley Centre
Epsom, Surrey

Tel: 01372-728520
Open: Mon-Sat 9.00-17.30
Sun 10.00-17.00

The frozen and chilled counter has pastries, sosage rolls, but no sandwiches.

---

213 High Street, Sutton,
Surrey SN1 1LB

Tel: 020-8642-5435
Open: *Mon-Sat* 9.00-17.30,
Sun 11.00-16.00

Limited fresh take-away like pies and pasties, some vegan. Also frozen/chilled section.

1098-99 The Mall
Whitgift Centre, Croydon
Surrey CR0 1UU

Tel: 020-8681 5174
Open: *Mon-Fri* 9.00-18.00,
Thu till 20.00
Sat 8.30-18.00,
Sun 11.00-17.00

One of the larger stores with fresh take-away snacks, a big chilled and frozen section, supplements and toiletries.

12-13 Apple Market, Kingston
Surrey KT1 1JF

Tel: 020-8541-1378
Open: *Mon-Sat* 9.00-17.30
Sun 11.00-17.00

Fresh take-away snacks available, some of which may be vegan like pasties and pies. There is a chiller section and frozen food.

50a George St, Richmond
Surrey TW9

Tel: 020-8940 1007
Open: *Mon-Sat* 9.00-17.30
Sun 11.30-16.30

Fresh take-away snacks as well as the usual health foods and supplements. Chilled and frozen foods.

WEST LONDON

Organic Café

Vegetarian English and Thai Cafe

The Auction Rooms
71 Lots Road, Chelsea
London SW10
Tel: 020-7351 7771

Open: *Sun*   10.00-18.30
Tube: Fulham Broadway
No credit cards. No smoking.
Children welcome.

Veggie cafe at the back of an
auction room offering a very
different Sunday out. It's
inside the auction rooms
where antiques are being
sold, and it cannot be seen
from the street. English and
Thai dishes prepared by the
vegan Thai proprietor Vip.
Most food is wheat free.

Main course £4, salad £3,
main course and salad £6.
Try Thai stir-fry rice noodles
(pad Thai), Thai rice and veg
curry, hot pot, moussaka,
vegan spicy samosas.

Organic sandwiches. Soup £3
with organic bread.

Organic teas, coffee and
alternatives £1. Freshly made
real fruit juice.

Organic cakes, some vegan,
such as chocolate almond
£1.90, flapjacks or brownies
£1.20.

Wagamama Kensington

Omnivorous Japanese

Lower Ground Floor,
Harvey Nichols
109-125 Knightsbridge

Tel: 020-7201 8000
Open: *Mon-Sat* 12.00-23.00
          Sun   12-22.00
Tube: Knightsbridge

Omnivorous   fast   food
Japanese noodle bar with
over nine veggie and vegan
dishes.For   menu   see
Bloomsbury, Central London.

Greens Foods

Health food shop & take-away

11-13 Strutton Ground
off Victoria Street
London SW1P
Tel: 020-7222 4588

Open: *Mon-fri* 8.30-17.30
          Sat-Sun closed
Tube: St James's Park

One of the largest health
food stores in London,
established 19 years, with
lots of take-away food,
situated midway between
Victoria Station & The House
of Commons. Nearby are
Buckingham Palace and St
James's Park, where you
could take some of their food
for a picnic.

Wholesome and tasty foods covering a broad range of special diets. Take-away or heat up there 50p-£3, ranging from sandwiches, ready made meals such as curries, salads, pasta dishes, Mediterranean, Thai and Middle Eastern. Vegan cakes sliced or whole.

Lots of supplements, herbals, homeopathic, sports and nutrition, essential oils and flower remedies. Extensive range of gluten free and wheat free products, toiletries and books. In store homeopath/herbalist/nutritionist/aromatherapist for consultation or advice on special diets.

Health Craze SW5

Health food shop

115 Earls Court Road
Earls Court
London SW5
Tel: 020-7244-7784

Open:

Mon–fri	10.00–23.00
Sat	11–23.00
Sun	14.00–23.00

Tube: Earls Court

Health food shop that has similar range to their sister shop in Old Brompton Road but no take-away.

Health Craze SW7

Health food shop & take-away

24 Old Brompton Rd.
South Kensington
London SW7
Tel: 020-7589-5870

Open:

Mon–fri	8.45–19.45
Sat	9.30–18.00
Sun	closed

Health food shops with plenty of take-away food like sandwiches, pasties and samosas, also mobile munchies like dried fruit, nuts and seeds. Good selection of cruelty-free cosmetics like Weleda and Dead Sea Magik.

Health Foods

Health food shop & take away

767 Fulham Road
London SW6
Tel: 020-7736 8848

Open:

Mon–Sat	9.00–17.30
Sun	closed

Health food shop with take-away snacks, some vegan. They have a freezer section with vegan ice-cream. Cruelty free toiletries like Dead Sea Magik. Also books.

Top homeopathic practitioner available by appointment on Tuesday and

Thursday mornings. Kinesiologist on Friday. 10% discount to senior citizens Thurday and Friday, and for everyone Saturday 9–10a.m.

Connected to the Aetherius Society.

Montignac Boutique
Wholefood shop and café

160 Old Brompton Rd
South Kensington
London SW5
Tel: 020-73702010
Open:

Mon–fri	8.30–21.00
Sat	8.30–18.00
Sun	10.00–18.00

Wholefood shop and café since 1994, with nothing refined, no sugar, adhering to the 'Montignac method', the original low glycaemic (GI) destination long before Gillian McKeith.

Freshly cooked daily hot and cold take-away with some choices for veggies and vegans. It's not all veggie.

Queens Health Shop
Health food shop

64 Gloucester Road
London SW7 4QT
Tel: 020-7584-4815

Open:

Mon–fri	9.00–18.30
Sat	9.00–17.30
Sun	closed

Health food shop with large selection of vitamins, skin-care and body products, also organic ranges and pre-packed veggie/vegan food to take away such as muesli, flapjacks and chocolate, but no fresh food available.

Revital Health Place
Health food shop

3a The Colonnades
123–151 Buckingham Palace Rd
London SW1W
Tel: 020-7976-6615
Open:

Mon–fri	9.00–19.00
Sat	9.00–18.00
Sun	closed

Tube: Victoria

Health food shop between Victoria coach and train station with macrobiotic foods and a large range of sea vegetables. Also vegan desserts, pasties, pizza and cakes. Nelsons products and lots of books. Organic cosmetics, herbs and supplements. A great place to stock up before a coach journey. Nutritionist based at shop on Wednesdays.

Planet Organic

Wholefood supermarket & veg. cafe

25 Effey Road
Fulham, London SW6
Tel 020-7731 7222

Open: Mon–Fri 8.30–20.30
Sat 10.00–18.00
Sun 12.00–18.00

Tube: Fulham Broadway
No smoking
Visa, MC

The third Planet Organic, opened in 2004 just a minute from Fulham Broadway underground. The groceries section has all organic fruit and veg. Health and bodycare has qualified staff to advise you including a nutritionist and a herbalist to explain the vitamins, herbs, tinctures, floral essences, aromatherapy and homeopathy. Lots of books about health and bodycare.

The vegetarian café section is open throughout the day and all ingredients come from the shop. Eat in or out, hot and cold and salad, mix what you want. Small box £2.25, medium £4, large £5. Small platter £5.50, big one £7. All organic cakes, 50% vegan.

Juice bar with smoothies £3, juices £2.60–2.80. Cappuccino £1.75, and three kinds of soya milk including vanilla.

North End Road Market

Street market

South end of North End Road below Lillie Road

Open: Mon–Sat 7.00–17.00
Thu 7.00–13.00
Sun 11.00–17.00

Tube: Fulham Broadway

Loads of fruit and veg stalls along the side of the road which is not pedestrianised though the traffic moves slowly towards the Fulham Broadway roundabout. Just past there is the brand new Planet Organic store, with a brilliant cafe area to tank up after doing the market.

Lush Victoria

Cruelty-free cosmetics

Unit 42, Platforms 15–18,
Victoria Rail Station,
115 Buckingham Palace Rd
London SW1V 9SJ
Tel: 020-7630 9927

Open: Mon–Thu 8.00–20.00
Fri 10.00–19.00
Sat 10.00–19.00
Sun 12.00–19.00

Tube: Victoria

Hand-made cosmetics, 70% of them vegan.

193

Holland & Barrett

Health food shop

Unit 15, Victoria Place Shopping
Ctr, Buckingham Palace Rd
London SW1W 9SA
Tel: 020-7828-5480

Open: *Mon–fri* 8.00–20.00
Sat 9.00–19.00
Sun 11.00–17.00

Tube: Victoria

Health food store at the back
of Victoria rail station
upstairs in the shopping
centre where you can stock
up on the way to the National
Express and Eurolines coach
station. There is a
Sainsbury's supermarket
opposite and a branch of
Books Etc nearby for your
travel guides.

220 Fulham Rd
London SW10 9NB
Tel: 020-7352 9939

Open: *Mon–fri* 9.30–18.00
Sat 9.30–5.30
Sun closed

Health food store with lots
of supplements and snacks

10 Warwick Way
Pimlico
London SW1V 1QT
Tel: 020-7834-4796

Open: *Mon–Sat* 9.00–18.00
Sun closed

Wide range of supplements
but no take-away.

192 Earls Court Rd
London SW5 9QF
Tel: 020-7370 6868

Open: *Mon–Sat* 9.00–19.00
Sun 11–16.00

Health food store with lots
of veggie snacks and fridge
with pastries etc.

73 Kings Road
Chelsea
London SW3 4NX
Tel: 020-7352 4130

Open: *Mon–Sat:* 9.00–19.00
Sun: 11.00–18.00

As well as the usual foods,
this store also offers monthly
allergy testing. Call ahead.

260 High Street
Kensington
London W8 6NA
Tel: 020-7603 2751

Open: *Mon–Sat* 9.00–17.30
closed Sun

Tube: High St. Kensington

Small health food store with
no fridge so no take-aways.

139 Church St
Kensington
London W8 7EN
Tel: 020-7727 9011

Open: *Mon–Sat* 9.00–18.00
Sun closed

Small health food store with
no fridge so no take-aways.

HAMMERSMITH
West London

Hammersmith might at first glance seem like a huge round-about under a giant flyover. However as well as being an important conference and business centre, there are fabulous walks by the peaceful Thames, some great British pubs, and the Riverside Studios for arty cinema and theatre. Nearby Shepherds Bush Green has the Bush Theatre where many top music acts perform.

There are terrific vegetarian dining possibilities. The Gate (below) and Blah Blah Blah are two of London's longest established vegetarian restaurants. Sagar is a newish Indian restaurant. Nearby, the big new winter 2004 opening was 222 at 222 North End Road. Co-founder Ben Asamani has been head chef at both Country Life and Plant. The initial menu was compiled as we went to press and our spies got down there and report it's every bit as good as it sounds, especially for the desserts. Unlike many vegan restaurants, this one serves alcohol.

The Gate

International vegetarian restaurant

Open:

Mon–Sat 12.00–15.00
18.00–23.00
(last orders)
Sun closed
Book at least 2 days ahead at the weekend:
hammersmith@gateveg.co.uk

51 Queen Caroline St
Hammersmith, London W6 9QL
Tel: 020–8748 6932
Tube: Hammersmith
Kids welcome, high chairs.
Visa, MC. Smoking allowed.
Menus at www.gateveg.co.uk

Top class international vegetarian restaurant. A finalist for the Vegetarian Society's best gourmet UK vegetarian restaurant of 2004 and popular with famous veggies. Unique setting in an artist's studio with modernist leanings. Many vegan and gluten-free options, cleared marked on the menu, which changes frequently with the seasons.

Nine starters, most vegan or can be, £2.25–£5.50 like marinated Greek olives, soup of the day, beetroot and horseradish potato cake, sweetcorn fritters, warm root vegetable salad, Indian pancake. Mezze platter £12.50 (serves 2) with a selection of all starters.

5 mains, 4 vegan or vegan option, £10–11.75, such as wild mushroom rosti, a celeriac and potato rosti served on a bed of pan-fried Savoy cabbage, topped with sauteed girolles, pied blue, oyster and horse mushrooms, finished with a whiskey cep sauce; mussamen curry with pumpkin, baby onions, baby corn, mange-tout and pineapple cooked in a richly spiced coconut sauce, served with wild and basmati rice and a paw-paw salsa; aubergin teriyaki; tortillas. Pasta of the day. Side orders like rocket salad, French beans or roast potatos £2.95–3.75.

Seasonal specials like the autumn 6 course fungi menu £35. 7 desserts, 2 or 3 vegan or vegan options, £3.95–6.00, such as apple and blackberry charlotte.

Extensive wine menu divided into red and white, light and medium, full bodied. House wine £10.50 bottle, £3 glass. Dessert wine £3.50–4.95.

Coffees, teas and herb teas £1.25–1.75, can do decaffeinated or with soya milk.

Open:
Every day 12–15.30
17.30–22.30
Children welcome, high chairs on the way. Visa, MC. Fully licensed.

222 North End Road
London W14 9NU
Tel: 020-7381 2322
Tube: West Brompton, West Kensington, Fulham Broadway

London's newest gourmet vegan restaurant, opened December 2004. Head chef Ben Asamani previously ran the kitchens at Country Life and Plant and offers outstandingly tasty and healthy cuisine with vegan desserts to die for. Lunchtime buffet, evening a la carte.

Starters £3.25–4.50 include soup; avocado with tomato sauce and vegan cream; black eye bean and tofu pate pancake with tomato chunks and cream sauce; pitta with dips; baked mushrooooms in extra virgin olive oil with special oatmeal on a bed of salad with tartar saruce.

Main courses £7.50–10.50 such as marinated organic tofu baked in oat crumbs on tomato wholemeal spaghetti; 222 Gardens, eastern meets Afro-Carib with plantain, okra, falafels, tomato salsa, baked aubergines, courgettes and crispy garlic bread; Seitan Stroganoff; Broccolini di Parma pancakes stuffed with tofu cottage cheese and pimento sauce; pasta with wild mushrooms and leek, in lime and garlic with cashew cream; chef's seasonal salad; Ben's Special West Indian stir-fry.

Side dishes £1.50–2.20 include garlic bread, yam, baked plantain. Salads £1.95–4.25 include mixed leaf; broccoli and mushroom; roast courgettes and aubergines; tomato, tofu and cucumber; Jerusalem artichokes and sundried tomatoes.

Desserts include organic vegan ice-cream, tofu cheesecake with warm vanilla soya dessert or ice-cream, organic cakes, pancakes with warm vanilla and chocolate sauce, mango sorbet, £2.95–4.50.

Service not included, discretionary 12.5% added to tables of 6 or more. 10% discount for Vegetarian and Vegan Society members. Outside catering.

Blah Blah Blah

Vegetarian restaurant

78 Goldhawk Road
Shepherds Bush, W12 8HA
Tel: 020 8746 1337

Open: *Mon-Sat* 12.00-14.30
19.00-23.00
Sun closed

Tube: Shepherds Bush
Cash or cheque.
Bring your own alcohol.
Non smoking area.

Vegetarian restaurant on two floors near Shepherds Bush Green. International menu. One starter and one main dish are always vegan and they can sometimes veganize certain dishes.

At least two hot or cold starters £3.95-4.95 like rolled aubergine kofta, mushroom galette with white wine sauce, mushroom and aubergine timbali, salads, soup of the day.

Five main courses £9.95 such as Thai green curry with basmati rice and fruit salsa; vegetable pie and chips with onion gravy .

Four desserts £4.95, always at least one vegan such as summer pudding. (Fantastic, we've waited ten years for this! Expect an influx of vegans.)

No booze so bring your own and pay £1.25 corkage per person. NB: no credit cards.

Sagar

Indian vegetarian restaurant

157 King St, Hammersmith W6
Tel: 020-8741 8563

Open: *Mon-Fri* 12-14.45
17.30-22.45
Sat-Sun 12-22.45

Tube: Hammersmith
Smoking area. Visa, MC, Amex. Children welcome, one baby chair, kids' dishes.

South Indian vegetarian restaurant near the Town Hall. Thali set meal £11.45 with starters, curries and dessert.

Some vegan food as they use both vegetable or butter ghee in different dishes, and they have vegan mango sorbet dessert. Some children's dishes too.

Wine £2.25-2.50 glass, £10-22 bottle.

Bushwacker Wholefoods

wholefood shop

132 King Street,
Hammersmith, London W6 OQU
Tel: 020-8748-2061

Open: *Mon–Sat* 9.30–18.00
      Tues   10.00–18.00
Sun & bank holidays closed

Tube: Hammersmith

Vegetarian wholefood shop that is completely GMO free. Plenty for vegans, as well as organic fruit and veg. Speciality product ranges include macrobiotic and gluten-free.

Non-dairy cheese, ice-cream. Household, skin and body-care, books, natural remedies and aromatherapy oils. Curent campaigning issues in the window such as GM and the supplements directive.

Holland & Barrett

Health food store

Unit 5, Kings Mall, King St
Hammersmith, London W6 0DP
Tel: 020-8748 9792

Open: *Mon–Sat* 9.00–18.00
      Sun   11.00–16.00

Tube: Hammersmith

A few take-aways like soya sausage rolls. Non-dairy ice-cream.

112 Shepherds Bush Centre
Shepherds Bush, W12 5PP
Tel: 020-8743 1045

Open: *Mon–Sat* 9.30–18.00
      Sun   11.00–16.00

Tube: Shepherds Bush

Health food store opposite the Central Line tube station with some take-away savouries like soya sausage rolls. Vegan ice-cream.

WEMBLEY West London

Wembley is home to a large Indian community and you won't be disappointed by the huge selection of food available here, whether you come for the Sunday market or a concert or conference. Head down Wembley High Road and Ealing Road for stacks of Gujarati and other Indian vegetarian cafes and restaurants with heaps of gastronomic sensations.

Long established favourites include Woodlands, Chetna's, Sakonis (now serving breakfast, also Chinese dishes) and Maru's (Indian and Kenyan Asian). There are several newer places too including Chowpatty , Hotel Sarabhavan, Sarash-wathy Bavans and a vegetarian pizza parlour.

While Wembley Stadium is being rebuilt, the big Sunday market (09.00–14.00) has moved to the car park near Wembley Arena, on the corner of Olympic Way and Engineers Way.

Chetna's

Gujarati and South Indian restaurant

420 High Road
Wembley
Middlesex HA9 6AH
Tel: 020-8903 5989

Open: *Mon*   closed
          Tues-Fri 12.00–15.00 &
                    18.00–22.30
          Sat-Sun 13.00–22.30

Tube: Wembley Central
MC, Visa, Amex. No smoking
Children welcome, 5 high chairs

Gujarati and South Indian vegetarian restaurant with take-away service specializing in Indian snacks, dosas, simple curries and pizzas. Affordable food and highly recommended by the Young Indian Vegetarians.

All the usual Indian starters (15 in all) such as bhelpoori, pani poori, dahi bateta poori or aloo tiki £2.40–2.80

Plenty of choice of dosas, all under £5, like plain £3, paper dosa served with vegetable sambhar £4.40, masala £3.70. If you fancy a change from the usual Indian fare you can also get a large vegetarian deep pan pizza (can be without cheese) or a hot and spicy one from £6.70 with a choice of toppings and extras.

There is a range of veggie desserts but nothing vegan.

Several wines and a selection of beers including Kingfisher. House wine £2 glass, £6.95 bottle.

Minimum charge of £5.50 per person.

Chowpatty

Vegetarian Indian restaurant

234 Ealing Road
Wembley
Middlesex HA0 4QL
Tel: 020 8795 0077

Open: *Mon-Sat* 10.00–22.00

Tube: Alperton, Wembley Central
Visa, MC

Named after Mumbai's famous beach, this is a new vegetarian restaurant in a road where the pickings for vegetarians were already far from slim (although the newcomers are always welcome). The prices are cheap and the variety good. You can get a lunchtime thali for £3.99 which includes a dal, two vegetable dishes, chappatis, rice and pickle; and you can choose from south, east or north Indian for a main.

Starters, £1.45–£2.95, with chaats, bhel puri and paani

puri.

Mains, £2.75–£4.95, such as rajma chawal (red kidney beans with rice) from Punjab in the north, idli and dosas from south India, or Indo-Chinese offerings in the form of noodles or Chinese idli. Worth a mention too are the lemon or coconut rice, £1.99.

Drinks from £1.25, with delicious sweet or salted lime soda at £1.95. Beers £2.75. House wine £6.95 for a bottle.

Hotel Sarabhavan

South Indian vegetarian restaurant

533 Wembley High Road
Wembley
Middlesex HA0 2DJ

Open: Mon–Sun 11.00–23.00
Tube: Wembley Central

South Indian vegetarian restaurant replacing 'Ahimsa' and opening at the end of Nov 2004. No telephone number available at time of going to press.

Jashan

Gujarati Indian restaurant

1–2 Coronet Parade
Ealing Road
Wembley, Middlesex HA0 4AY
Tel: 020-8900-9800

Open: Mon–Fri 12.00–15.30
         18.00–23.00
         Sat–Sun 12.00–23.00

Tube: Wembley Central, Alperton
Alcohol and smoke free zone.
Children welcome, high chairs.
www.jashanrestaurants.com

South Indian and Chinese vegetarian restaurant which aims to "promote healthy vegetarian food, that's rightly spiced and less oily". The menu has 13 different sections and stacks of veggie snacks.

Vegetarian specialities include bharwan bhindi, pakoda kadhi or jeera aloo for £3.50. Then there are 'treasures of the Nawabs': subzi pulao or saade chawal for £3.95 each. "Tangy bites" include aloo tikkiya chaat or karol baug ke samose at £3.95. Mumbai Express section has a Bombay burger for £3.25.

Classics such as veg biriyani are also available here, noodles and of course rice. Lots of Indian breads like paratha, tandoori roti, masala kulchi for around £1.50–£1.95.

Many cold drinks like fresh coconut water and fresh lime juice with soda water.

They have outside seating in the summer for around 25 people.

Maru's Bhajia House

Vegetarian Indian café

230 Ealing Road
Alperton, Wembley
Middlesex HA0 4QL
Tel: 020 8903 6771
Open: *Mon–Thu* 12.30–20.30
　　　　Fri–Sun 12.30–21.30
Tube: Alperton,Wembley Central
MC, Visa, Amex
No alcohol.
Children welcome, high chair
www.mambhajia.com

Ealing Road has a number of inexpensive Gujarati and south Indian restaurants. Maru's Kenyan Asian cuisine has been a firm favourite since 1976 with bhajias of course, samosas, maize and assorted snacks. Before that the family had a restaurant in East Africa from 1949 to 1972.

The Maru bhajia has always been the main item on the menu, made from potato slices mixed with gram (chickpea) flour fried with spices, with their special tamarind sauce.

Asian film stars fill up here on pani puri, kachori and vada. £3.40 for a portion, £6.80 for a double portion.

Desserts include fruit cocktail. Fresh passion fruit juice £3.

This is a café with seating for 30 to 34 people and gets very busy.

Naklank Sweet Mart

Gujarati Indian café take–away

50b Ealing Road
Wembley, Middlesex HA0 4TQ
Tel: 　　020–8902 8008
Open:
Mon–Sat 10.30–19.00
Sun 　　12.00–19.00
Tube: Wembley Central
　　　　Alperton

Alcohol and smoke free zone.
Children welcome.

Gujarati vegetarian Indian eat in or take–away. Everything made on the premises with 39 different sweets and savouries, samosas, pakoras, 20 kinds of bhajia. Curries from £2.50 and mostly vegan. All traditionally made. Small seating area with two tables inside. Outside catering service.

Pizza Parlour

Vegetarian pizza restaurant

218 Ealing Road, Wembley
Tel: 020-8900 9999
Open: *Tue-Fri* 12.00-15.00
                    17.00-22.00
         Sat-Sun 13.00-22.00
Mon (except bank hol) Closed
Tube: Wembley Central, Alperton
MC, Visa

Vegetarian pizzas from £3.50, side dishes such as potato wedges and masala or chilli chats from £1.50. Eat in or take away.

Wine from £2 for a glass, £12.99 for a bottle. Beers £2.30.

Sakonis

Indian restaurant and take-away

127-129 Ealing Road
Wembley, Middlesex HA0 4BP
Tel: 020-8903-9601 / 1058
Open:
Every day breakfast 08.00-11.00
         (*weekend* 9-11.00)
Summer
         Sun-Thu 12-22.00
         Fri-Sat 12-22.30
Winter
         Sun-Thu 12-21.30
         Fri-Sat 12-22.00
Tube: Wembley Central, Alperton

Vegetarian Indian snack bar, take-away and delivery service with an extensive menu of over 100 Gujarati, North Indian and Chinese dishes.

Buffet south Indian breakfast weekdays 8-11am for £3, weekends 9-11 £3.50, eat as much as you like with idli, mini dosas, lots of good stuff and tea.

Buffet lunch every day 12-16.00, eat as much as you like for £5.99. 10% eat in charge added to bill.

Buffet dinner every day 19-21.30, £7.99 + 10%.

Starters £1.50-£3.95 such as sev puri, pani puri, samosas, toasted sandwiches, spring rolls, khichi (rice flour steamed with spices) or pancake made from gram flour.

Main dishes £3.50–£6.50 such as plain and Mysore masala dosa, farari cutlets, vegetable biriyani, corn bhaji, veggie burger and chips, chow mein with Haka noodles and fried veg, Szechuan spicy noodles, aubergine and chilli in hot black bean sauce. Manchow soup £2.75.

Lots of sweets, fruit shakes and fresh juices from £2.75, including fresh coconut water.

Take-away Indian sweet shop too.

Sarashwathy Bavans

South Indian vegetarian restaurant

549 High Road
Wembley
Middlesex HA0 2DJ
Tel: 020 8902 1515
Open: *Mon–Sun* 12.00–23.00
Tube: Wembley Central
www.sarashwathy.com
Visa, MC (minimu £10)
No alcohol. Children welcome, high chair

South Indian fare and Indo–Chinese choices. This is a new and popular place which offers free delivery within a 3 mile radius (minimum order of £12) and outside catering orders. Starters, £1.75–£5.25, with samosas, soups and vegetable rolls; mains from £3.95 with large selection of dosas, idli and noodles. Fresh juices from £1.95.

Tulsi

22/22A Ealing Road
Wembley HA0 4TL

Tel: 020-8900 8526

Open: *Tue–Fri* 11.00–15.00
                   18.00–22.30
      Sat–Sun 11.00–22.30
      Mon   closed

Tube: Wembley Central
tulsirestaurant@yahoo.co.uk

South Indian place with Indo-Chinese offerings. Staples such as idli and several types of dosa – plain, masala and even noodles dosa, from £3. Variety of soups from £2.50. Vegetable dishes from £3.70 and fried rice, noodles and chow mein from £4. Prices £2–3.00.

Woodlands

402a High Road
Wembley
Middlesex HA9 9LH

Tel: 020-8902 9869
Open:
Every day 12.00–15.00
          18.00–23.00

Tube: Wembley Central,
            Wembley Stadium

MC, Visa, Amex
No smoking
Children welcome, 2 high chairs
www.woodlandsrestaurant.co.uk

Long established vegetarian Indian restaurant, one of four in London serving classic Indian dishes. This branch is decorated in vibrant colours with a bright and airy feel.

Located within walking distance of Wembley conference centre, and 5 minutes from Wembley Central. This branch has regular changing specials. For more menu details see the Marylebone Road branch (Central London, page 68), though this one is a bit cheaper.

House wine £10, glass £2.25. Beer small (330ml) £2.75, large (660ml) £5.35.

Holland & Barrett

Health food shop

Unit 21 Wembley Sq, High Rd,
Wembley, Middlesex HA9 7AJ

Tel: 020-8902-6959
Open: *Mon–Sat* 9.00–17.30
         Sun   closed
Tube: Wembley Central,
         Wembley Stadium

They have a small take-away
section with pastries, plus
usual health foods, a chiller
cabinet and freezer section.

Sabras

South Indian Gujarati restaurant

Open:
Tue–Sun 18.30–23.30,
last orders 22.30, closed Mon
No smoking.
Children welcome, no high chairs.
Visa, MC. 12.5% service charge.

263 High Road
Willesden Green
London NW10 2RX
Tel: 020-8459-0340
Tube: Willesden Green, Dollis Hill. Close to Willesden bus garage.

Willesden & Kilburn

Vegetarian and 75% organic South Indian and Gujarati restaurant, with some North Indian dishes too. Specialists in Surati (pronounced hurti) cuisine. Around 50 items on the huge menu, almost all of them vegan, and they can cater for wheat-free and Jains. They specialise in the use of ground nut oil, fresh ginger, chilli, garlic, lemon, coconut and coriander. Over 20 award certificates on the walls – if you want outstanding Indian food, go to Sabras. While everyone else in London has been pumping up prices since our last edition, Sabras have held theirs and even reduced some. Family-run since 1973 by the proprietor-manager Hermant Desai and his wife Nalinee who is the head chef.

7 starters, all vegan, £3.50, such as bhel puri, sev puri, pani puri, samosas, chana dal steam cooked, fried banana balls.

10 kinds of dosa £3.50–6.50, or have a small one as a starter. These are south Indian pancakes filled with vegetables and spices and make a complete meal. All kinds of Indian vegetable and lentil dishes £4.90–5.50 like sweet potato, Kashmiri kofta, spinach palak with spices, steamed chick pea and potato with ginger, mixed lentils and beans. Fill up with thin chapatis or thick paratha bread, which can be stuffed with vegetables.

Two of the four desserts are vegan, either chilled mango pulp or puran-poli, a mini chupati filled with sweetened Toover dal, enriched with nutmeg, cloves and cardamon, £3.50.

Two page drinks menu including house wine £2.50 glass, £9.50 bottle. Beer £2.75. Coffee or pot of tea £1.50.

Hugo's Restaurant

Open:
Mon–Sat 9.30–23.00

MC, Visa,12.5% service charge.
Children welcome, high chairs

25 Lonsdale Road
Queens Park
London NW6 6RA
Tel: 020-7372 1232
Tube: Queen's Park

Organic omnivorous restaurant. 50% veggie global menu using fresh seasonal produce. They don't use any animal fat in cooking or preparation of food. Some of the veggie options may be vegan, but we advise vegans to check by phone first as the menu differs every day.

They offer a full English veggie (can be vegan) breakfast for £6.80, or pancake with maple syrup and/or fruit salad.

Lunch served from 12.30–16.00 with daily special on the board, £2–£12, e.g. veg stir fry with brown rice £7.80, herb risotto £7.80, big soup £4.50.

The evening menu has a set platter for veggies which included a starter of wild mushroom risotto with truffle oil for £6.80. The main course £11.80 was either chilli tofu with tempura of vegetables and quinoa with sesame dressing; or courgette timbale with roast beetroot, braised fennel and walnut oil with balsamic vinaigrette. Various side dishes at £3.80 each.

Desserts £5.50 and cakes £2–£4.50 such as vegan chocolate or lemon polenta.

House wine £2.80 glass, £9.80 bottle.

Bhavna Sweet Mart

Indian veggie & vegan take-away

237 High Road
Willesden
London NW10
Tel: 020-8459 2516
Open: *Every day* 10.00-20.00
Tube: Willesden Grn, Dollis Hill

Indian vegetarian and vegan take-away with 7 seats. Sweets, large portions of curry with rice, naan, parathas, bhajias etc.

Don't get there too late in the day in case all the best stuff's been scoffed, or order some food by phone.

They are also open on Christmas Day if you feel like something different!

Kua Siam

Omnivorous Thai restaurant

265 High Road
Willesden
London NW10 2RX
Tel: 020-8451 1276
Open: *every day* 18.30-24.00
Wed-Mon 10.00-20.00
Tube: Dollis Hill

New omnivorous Thai restaurant next door to Sabras in premises that used to be an Indian sweet mart. Vegetarian dishes include red or green curry, stir-fried veg with oyster mushroom sauce, Pad Thai noodles with veg, sweet and sour veg, tofu. During the daytime it's a Thai cafe with different owners.

Saravanas

South Indian vegetarian restaurant

77-81 Dudden Hill Lane
London NW10 1BD
Tel: 020-8459 4900
Open: *Tue-Sun* 12.00-22.30
Mon closed
Tube: Dollis Hill
Children welcome, high chairs
Visa, MC. No smoking.

New Indian vegetarian restaurant just up the road from Sabras. Buffet lunch £4.75.

Human Nature

Health food store & take-away

25 Malvern Road
London NW6
Tel: 020-7328 5452
Open: *Mon-Fri* 9.00-18.00
Sat 9.00-17.00
Sun closed

Health food store where the

take-away selection has an Eastern slant, and they stock most other veggie foods and household products and toiletries. Quite a lot of take-away food including cottage pies, rolls, falafel, meals with rice, spring rolls, samosas, pastries. Constantly changing, always something new.

The manager, Mr Nari Sadhuram, sells veggie remedies for various maladies such as jet-lag and hangovers, and is also a trained masseur so you can have a Swedish or an Indian head massage or make an appointment for a home visit.

Meeras Health Food Ctr.

Health food shop

Health food shop
2 High Street
Harlesden
London NW10 4LX
Tel: 020-8965 7610
Open: *Mon-Sat* 10.00-18.00
Sun closed

Heath food shop with vitamins and supplements. Freezer with soya ice-cream. Free advice on products.

No fresh take-away but they have dried fruits, nuts and seeds, flapjacks.

Mistry

Health Food Shop & Pharmacy

16-20 Station Parade
Willesden Green
London NW2 4NH
Tel: 020-8450 7002
Open: *Mon-Sat* 9.30-19.00
Tube: Willesden Grn.

Health food shop with pharmacy and two homeopaths next door. Take-away food includes sandwiches, salads, samosas, burgers etc. with lots for vegans. Reflexology, optician, acupuncture and massage offered.

Olive Tree

Vegetarian wholefood shop

84 Willesden Lane
London NW6 7TA
Tel: 020-7328 9078
Open: *Mon-Sat* 10.00-18.30
Wed 13.00-19.00
Sun closed

Vegetarian wholefood shop with lots of snacks for veggies and vegans. Flower remedies, vitamins and supplements.

Take-away selection includes rolls and sandwiches and some meals. Large selection of fresh organic fruit and veg. All displayed in a charming old worldly style wooden interior.

Revital Health Shop

Health food shop

35 High Road
Willesden NW10
Tel: 020-8459-3382

Open: *Mon–Sat* 9.30–19.00
Sun 11.00–16.00

Tube: Willesden Green

Fridge and freezer section, take-away food includes pies and pasties, many of them vegan. Lots of vitamins and minerals and the nutritionist on site gives free advice on supplements.

Mail order with freephone number 0800-252875.

Chai

Vegetarian/vegan
Chinese restaurant

Open:

Mon–Fri	12–14.30 & 18–23.30
Sat	12–15.30 & 18–23.30
Sun	12.00–23.30

Visa, MC

Smoking area at back.

236 Station Road
Edgware
Middlesex HA8 7AU

Tel: 020–8905 3033

Tube: Edgware

Almost entirely vegan Chinese restaurant, Buddhist owned, now with a bar. They specialize in an astonishing range of fake meats and lots of other dishes. The ideal night out for both reluctant and avid vegetarians, with 153 items on the menu.

Lunch buffet Mon–Sat £4.50, Sun (12–4pm) £6.90.

23 appetizers £1.50 to £4 such as tempura, sesame toasts and seven kinds of soup.

You will be spoilt for choice with 23 middle courses £5.50–6.00 such as broccoli, quick fried with garlic sauce; satay with chopped onions and peppers in peanut sauce; sea spiced aubergine; French beans in black bean sauce. Lots of tofu dishes like ginger tofu, kung po tofu (deep fried with chestnuts), ma po tofu diced with Szechuan cabbage, onions, ginger and chillis stir fried in a hot sauce. Or you could be tempted by the aromatic crispy veg–duck with pancakes with hot hoi sin sauce, cucumber and spring onion for £6.00. Lots of noodle and rice dishes too.

2 set meals £12 or £15 per person.

Now serving liqueurs alcohol. Wine £2.50 glass, £9.50–14.50 bottle.

Advance booking required for big parties such as birthdays when they'll do somrthing special for you like a free dessert with a candle.

Free delivery within a three mile radius.

Jays Pure

Open:
Open 365 days a year
12.30–23.00
Visa, MC.
No smoking. No alcohol.
Children welcome, 2 high chairs.

547 Kingsbury Road
London NW9 9EL

Tel: 020-8204 1555
Tube: Kingsbury

Vegetarian restaurant, take-away & juice bar with a great menu and so much choice. Fast food but healthy with Indian, Chinese, Mexican and Thai menus. They use sunflower oil in cooking so many dishes are suitable for vegans.

Snacks or starters from £1.25 up to £6.50 including the usual Indian favourites and others, such as kachori (three piece turnover filled with dhal), corn bhaji, mogo chips, chilli mushroom, stir-fried aubergine or King Pow corn. There are also Thai dishes like Thai green curry, or Thai noodles priced at £3–£5.00.

Indian mains are all under £6.00 and include vegetable biriyiani and Hyderabad masala dosa.

Chinese curries such as baby corn with mushroom Szechuan style, aubergine black bean sauce, Manchurian cauliflower, all around £5.00.

The Mexican dishes are tortilla chips, tacos with chili bean and salad, burritos with picante sauce, Mexican rice and refried beans. These are £3 up to £6.00.

They also have 3 types of veggie burger and 7 types of noodles.

Indian desserts £3.60–5.00 but nothing vegan.

Fresh orange juice £2.75, passion fruit £3. Smoothies £2.75, but no soya milk.

Rose

Indian vegetarian

532–534 Kingsbury Road
London NW9 9HH
(near HSBC)

Tel: 020-8905 0035
Freephone 0800-583 8905

Open: *Every day* 12-22.30
Tube: Kingsbury

North and South Indian and
Chinese vegetarian restaurant and take-away. Gigantic
menu, over 100 dishes.
Excellent value. Buffet lunch
every day 12-15.00, £4.99.
No alcohol. No smoking.
Children welcome, high
chairs. MC, Visa

Gayatri Sweet Mart

Vegetarian take away

467 Kingsbury Road
Kingsbury, London NW9 9DY
Tel: 020-8206 1677

Open: *Mon-Fri* 10.30-18.30
     Sat   10.00-18.30
     Sun   9.00-16.00

Tube: Kingsbury

Indian vegetarian take-away.
46 dishes £7-£8 per kilo.
Savouries like samosa 45p,
bhajias, dhokra, kachori.
Sweets include barfis,
pendas, ladoos, chevda
(Bombay mix).

Diet & Health Centre

Health food shop

28 Watling Avenue
Burnt Oak
Edgware
Middlesex HA8

Tel: 020-8952-9629

Open: *Mon-Sat* 9.00-17.30
     Sun closed

Tube: Burnt Oak

Health food store. No fresh
take-away here but they do
have a good freezer section
with frozen meals. Also a
range of cruelty-free
toiletries.

Ram's Gujarati

Surti Cuisine Indian veggie

203 Kenton Road
Kenton, Harrow
Middlesex
Tel: 020-8907 2022
Open:
Every day 12-15.00 & 18-23.00
Tube: Kenton Rd 5 mins

Indian Gujarati vegetarian cuisine from the city of Surat. Around £8.99 for a thali with starter such as bhajias, papodoms, two curries, three djipatis, dal and dessert.

They use butter ghee, but vegetable ghee is available.

Desserts include vegan halva. Milkshakes can be made with soya milk.

Wine £2.10 glass, £9.20 bottle. Beer 330ml £1.50, 660ml £3.

All non-smoking. Wheelchair access and toilet. Visa, MC. Very child friendly, high chairs.

Pradip

Indian vegetarian restaurant & shop

154 Kenton Road
Kenton, Harrow
Middlesex HA3 8AZ

Tel: 020-8909 2232
shop 020-8907 8399
Open:

Restaurant
Tue-Sun   12-15.30
          18-22.00

Shop
Tue-Sat   10-19.00
Sun   9-17.00
closed Mon

Tube: Kenton Road
www.pradipsweet.co.uk

Indian vegetarian restaurant and sweet shop next door. They specialise is Punjabi food from the west of India. You can eat well here for under £10.

All day buffet Fri-Sun £7.90 includes starter, main course and soft drink. Also thalis from £4.90.

Being next to a sweet shop they're good at desserts, including Lebanese baklava, date rolls, vegan ladhu and coconut sweets.

They use vegetable ghee in cooking and butter ghee in sweets. Not licensed. No smoking. Visa, MC. Children welcome, 2 high chairs. Outside catering service. The restaurant takes party bookings of up to 110 people outside normal opening times.

Swadisht

Vegetarian Indian take-away

195 Streatfield Road
Kenton, Harrow
Middlesex
Tel: 020 8905 0202
Open: *Every day 12.30-22.30*
Tube: Kenton Road

New Indian vegetarian restaurant. A la carte, four people could have two courses for £30. No smoking, no alcohol. Children welcome, two high chairs. MC, Visa.

Natraj

Vegetarian Indian take-away

341 Northolt Road
South Harrow
Middlesex HA2 8JB
Tel: 020 8426 8903
Open:
Mon-Tue,
Thu-Sat   10.00-19.30
Sun   10-16.30
closed Wed
Tube: South Harrow

Indian vegetarian take-away with plenty for vegans. Starters/snacks such as bhajias, sweets, samosas etc.

Most curries are vegan such as spinach and chickpea,

okra and potato, cabbage and potato, soya bean, kidney bean and butterbean mix. A regular take-away box of curry is £2.50, large £3.50. Box of rice £1.50 and £2.50. Or get a box of half curry, half rice for £2 or £3, ideal for lunch.

Sakonis

Indian & Chinese restaurant

5-8 Dominion Parade
Station Road, Harrow
Middlesex HA1 2TR
Tel: 020-8863-3399
Open:
        Sun-Thu 12.00-21.30
        (last entry to restaurant)
        Fri-Sat 12.00-22.00
        Wed   closed
MC, Visa.
No alcohol. No smoking.
Children welcome, 7 high chairs.

Vegetarian Indian restaurant that also serves lots of Chinese dishes. Same menu as Wembley branch.

Bufet 12-3pm £6.50 + 10%, so £7.15 eat in (no take-away), 6.30-9.30pm £8.99 + 10%, i.e. £9.89. The buffet is a combination of the whole menu with 20 to 25 items including starters and 3 desserts.

Supreme Sweets

Indian vegetarian take-away.

706 Kenton Road, Kenton,
Harrow, Middlesex HA3 9QX

Tel: 020-8206 2212

Open:

Mon–Fri	10.00–19.00
Sat	9.30–19.00
Sun	8.30–17.30
closed Wed	

Tube: Kingsbury

Sweets and savouries like bhajias £7 per kilo, samosas and pakoras from 40p. Also frozen products like samosas, kachoris and spring rolls. 75% of items are vegan, vegetable oil in savouries but butter ghee in sweets. Catering for weddings and parties, they prepare for you to collect but deliver on orders over 100 people.

Holland & Barrett

Health food shop

22-24 College Road
Harrow, Middlesex HA1 1BE

Tel: 020-8427 4794

Open: Mon–Sat 9.00–17.30
  Sun 11–17.00

Health food shop with a few take-aways like pasties. Vegan ice-cream.

Veggie Inn

Health food shop

123 Headstone Road
Harrow HA1 1PG

Tel: 020-8863 6144

Open:
Wed–Mon 12.00–14.30
  1800–23.00
Tue closed

Tube: Harrow-on-the-Hill

Menu www.veggieinn.com

Really nice restaurant with almost 100 items on the menu including lots of fake meat dishes. Desserts include vegan ice-cream and banana fritters. Themed evenings, e.g. Valentine's. Free local delivery over £15.

Kathiyawadi

Vegetarian Gujarati restaurant

434 Rayners Lane
Pinner, Middlesex HA5 5DX

Tel: 020-8863 2723
  020-8868 9885

Open: *Mon–Fri* 17-23.00
  Sat–Sun 12-24.00

Tube: Rayners Lane

Average £10 for a good meal. Licensed. Children welcome, high chairs, MC, Visa. Smoking area.

Woodlands Chiswick

South Indian vegetarian

12–14 Chiswick High Road
London W4 1TH
Tel: 020-8994 9333

Open:
every day 12-14.45, 18-22.45

MC, Visa, Diners, Amex

Children welcome, high chairs

www.woodlandsrestaurant.co.uk

New branch of this excellent Indian vegetarian restaurant chain. For menu see Marylebone (page 68).

Shahanshah

North Indian veggie & vegan

60 North Road
Southall
Middlesex UB1 2JL
Tel: 020-8574-1493

Open: *every day* 10.00-20.00

Tube: Ealing Brdway, Southall BR
Children welcome, 2 high chairs

North Indian vegetarian restaurant, take-away and sweet centre with 50% of their ingredients organic.

Starters £1-1.25 such as two samosas eat in for £1, pakora £1. Main meal £5, eg curry and rice. Some food is vegan food as they use butter ghee, groundnut and sunflower oil.

Outside seating for 10 people and around 30 inside. Alcohol and smoke-free. No cards. They cater for parties and weddings.

The Grain Shop

Vegetarian bakery & take-away only

269a Portobello Road
Notting Hill, London W11
(In Portobello market, opposite Tavistock Rd)

Tel: 020-7229-5571

Open: *Mon-Sat* 9.30-18.00

Sun 11-16.30

Tube: Ladbroke Grove

Vegetarian take-away and bakery that uses organic flour. 16 hot dishes, 13 of which are suitable for vegans, like tofu stir-fry, veg curry or ratatouille, as well as salads all made on the premises. Small £2.25, medium £3.65, large £4.60.

Specialist breads and cakes for allergy free diets, also gluten-free pastries and sugar-free items.

Garden Café

Omnivorous café

The London Lighthouse
111-117 Lancaster Road
London W11
Tel: 020-7792 1200
Open: *Mon-Fri* 9-15.00
Sat-Sun closed
(occasionally open Sat)
Tube: Ladbroke Grove
No credit cards.
Smoking in garden.
Children welcome, but no high chairs.

Friendly omnivorous café, stylishly decorated, which always has some veggie meals, sometimes vegan. The London Lighthouse is a centre advising on HIV and the cafe is open to the public. On summer days the French windows open out onto a peaceful and relaxing, beautiful garden. Special days such as African when they always cater for veggies and vegans.

Good quality food at very reasonable prices with meals around £4, such as pasta, stuffed peppers or aubergine with rice or bulgur, served with veg. Salad bar with some vegan items at 60p per portion. Baked potatoes every day £2.50 with different fillings such as veggiemince, dairy-free broccoli mornay.

Freshly ground coffee, latte or large cappuccino £1.50, tea, juice, but no soya milk. (Usually when we say no soya milk, by the next edition there is!)

Kalamaras Restaurant

Greek omnivorous restaurant

66 Inverness Mews
Bayswater, London W2 3JQ
Tel: 020-7727 5082
Open:
Every day   12.00-15.00
17.00-24.00
(last order 23.00)
Tube: Bayswater, Queensway
Smoking & no smoking sections.
MC, Visa, Amex
Children welcome

Mediterranean Greek omnivorous taverna in a veggieless area on the north side of Hyde Park, close to Paddington Station. Vegetarians can try lots of starters for £3-3.50 such as aubergine dip or fresh artichoke hearts casseroled with broad beans and dill. In fact veggies and vegans can concoct a good meal of starters, or try the vegetarian moussaka £9.80, made with layers of sauteed potatoes, aubergines, courgettes and mushrooms topped with bechamel sauce which can be omitted for vegans for a bit less money.

Greek sweets for desserts, but all with honey.

Now licensed, house wine £10 bottle, £2.50 glass. Tea or filter coffee £1.50, no soya milk.

The Village

Indian omnivorous restaurant

Unit 1, Royale Leisure Park,
Kendal Avenue
(off Western Avenue (A40),
London W3 OPA

Tel: 020-8992 1212

Open: *Every day* 12.00-24.00

Tube: Park Royal

MC, Visa. Smoking section.

Children welcome, high chairs.

South Indian omnivorous restaurant, previously a vegetarian one called Indigo, in a complex with a cinema and bowling alley and a friendly lively atmosphere. The menu has South Indian offerings with dosas and noodles, £3-6.50, and Chinese veg and Hakka noodles £6.40. Lunchtime buffet £5.99 Mon-Fri 12.00-14.30.

Wok

Omnivorous Chinese restaurant

167 The Vale
Acton. London W3

Tel: 020-8740 0888

Open: *Mon-Fri* 12.00-22.00
Sat-Sun 13.00-22.00

Tube: Shepherds Bush

Omnivorous Chinese buffet restaurant west of Shepherds Bush where you can eat as much as you like for just £5. £3 or £4 for a take-away box. It used to be called Vegan Thai Buffet and is still half vegetarian with stir-fried rice, spring rolls, tofu, stir-fry veg, soya meats and noodles. A la carte mains £2.00-6.95.

As Nature Intended

Organic & health food shop

201 Chiswick High Road
Chiswick, London W4
Tel: 020-8742-8838

Open: *Mon–Fri*   9.00–20.00
        Sat   9.00–19.00
        Sun   11–17.30

Almost completely organic store that aims to combine the variety of a supermarket with the product range found in traditional health food shops. Many items are suitable for those with food allergies such as sugar-, gluten-, salt- or yeast-free. Bread and gluten-free muffins. Wide range including sandwiches and pies to take away.

Many tofu-based foods. Herbal and homeopathic remedies, aromatherapy oils, beauty and skincare products. Vitamins and minerals. Vegan and veggie wines are clearly labelled and there is a leaflet in case you're unsure what constitutes a vegan wine. Lots of books.

There are trained nutritionists and a herbalist in-house most afternoons for dietary advice. Certain days therapists offer treatments such as a free 15 miniute shiatsu, massage therapist, chiropractor.

Coltsfoot and Kelp

Wholefood shop

106 Northfields Avenue
London W13 9RT
Tel: 020-8567-3548

Open: *Mon–Sat* 9.30–17.30
       Sun closed
Tube: Northfields

No fresh take-away section but a well stocked freezer. They also have household products, body care, natiural remedies and homeopathic ranges. Ecover full range and refills.

Fresh & Wild

Organic supermarket & veggie cafe

210 Westbourne Grove
Notting Hill
London W11 2RH
Tel: 020-7229-1063

Open: *Mon –Sat*   8.00–21.00
       Sat   10–20.00
       Sun   10–19.00
Tube: Notting Hill Gate (7 min)

Huge wholefood and organic supermarket on three floors with a staggering array of foods from all over the world, lots of fruit and veg, wines and beers, take-away snacks, remedies, bodycare and books. Phenomenal, warm customer service with a passion for the environment and fully qualified nutritionists in health and bodycare.

Cafe area includes 25 seats inside and 12 on the pavement outside in exuberant, rich Notting Hill.

Breakfast includes vegan muesli, pain chocolat, fresh fruit salads, soya drinks.

Salad and hot food bar changes every day, £1.50 per 100 grammes, all fresh and seasonal. Try a shepherd's pie, coconut dahl, broccoli with steamed brown rice, or a daily chef's special such as nut roast.

Organic sandwiches just under £2. Huge range of wheat free organic pastries, muffins, 15 cakes of which a third to a half are now vegan. Tofu cheesecake.

Juice bar and smoothies £2.99, £3.99. Fair trade coffee, cappuccino £1.79, £2.00.

Gaia Wholefoods

Wholefood shop

123 St Margarets Road
Twickenham
Middlesex TW1 2LH

Tel: 0181-892 2262

Open: *Mon–Fri* 9.30-19.00
Sat: 17.00, *Sun closed*

Wholefood shop selling fresh organic fruit and vegetables, Japanese macrobiotics, organic bread. They stock body care, eco cleaning products and gluten free ranges. Also some vegan take-aways like pastries.

Health, My God Given Wealth

Wholefood shop

41 Turnham Green Terrace
London W4 1RG

Tel: 020-8995-4906

Open: *Mon–Fri* 9.30-18.30
Sat 9.30-17.30
Sun closed

Tube: Turnham Green

Quite a small wholefood shop but packed with hand-picked organic and natural products avoiding synthetic preservatives, that the staff use themselves like Dr Hauschka, Living Nature, Solgar, Biocare, Weleda, Barefoot Botanicals. Wide range of organic breads, dairy-free cheese, cream cheese and ice-cream. Frozen baby food. Natural remedies like Bioforce tinctures, Potters. Spirulina and green superfoods. Organic herbs and spices.

They plan to introduce a range of fresh take-away food. Fresh juices, guarana drinks.

Healthy Harvest Food Store

Wholefood shop

In Squires Garden Centre
6 Cross Road
Twickenham
Middlesex TW2 5PA
Tel: 020 7586 8012

Open: *Mon-Sat* 9.30–17.30
Sun 10.30–16.30

Get your gardening goodies and tank up on grub at this wholefood shop in a garden centre between Twickenham and Hampton Court. Usual foods plus serve yourself wholefoods. Vegetarian pasties and flapjacks. (Jus as well as the garden centre restaurant just does corpse and 2 veg.)

Holland & Barrett

Healthfood shop

32 Queensway
Bayswater
London W2 4QW
Tel: 020-7727 6449

Open: *Mon-Fri* 9.00–20.00
Sat 10.00–20.00
Sun 11.00–20.00

Tube: Queensway

Health food shop with some take-aways like pasties, but no sandwiches. Frozen foods including dairy-free ice-cream.

---

416 Chiswick High Rd
London W4 5TF
Tel: 020-8994–1683

Open: *Mon-Sat* 9.00–17.30
Sun 11.00–16.00

Small take-away section and some frozen food available at this store.

---

13 King St
Twickenham
Middlesex TW1 3SD
Tel: 020-8891–6696

Open: *Mon-Sat* 9.00–17.30
Sun closed

Fresh veggie take-away snacks like pies, pastries and soyos rolls arrive every Tuesday.

Luscious Organic

Organic food store

240–242 Kensington High St
London W8 6NE
(opposite Odeon cinema)
Tel: 020-7371 6987
Open: *Mon–Fri* 08.30–20.30
        Sat   09.00–21.00
        Sun   10.00–21.00
Tube: Earls Court, High St Ken

Big new organic food store,
predominantly vegetarian
apart from some baby foods.
Also cleaning products, a few
books (cooking, feng shui
etc), organic and vegetarian
wines.

A couple of hot dishes
£5.50, such as Moroccan
chickpea and spinach with
steamed brown rice and
salad. Soup with bread £4.
Take-away sandwiches.

Market Place

Vegetarian health food shop

8 Market Place
Acton, London W3
Tel: 020-8993-3848
Open: *Mon–Sat* 9.00–17.45
        Sun closed
Tube: Acton

Vegetarian health food shop,
with cosmetics and
aromatherapy supplies.
Impressive range of take-
away foods such as veggie
samosas, vegetable
couscous, chickpea salad,
rotis, spring rolls, organic
pies. Vegan ice-cream. Lots
of sports nutrition stuff.

Millenium Healthfoods

Health food shop

Unit 50b Ealing Broadway Centre
Ealing, London W5
Tel: 020-8840-6949
Open: *Mon–Sat* 9.00–18.00
        Sun   11.00–17.00

Health food shop with
supplements and whole-
foods. No fresh take away,
but has a freezer counter.
Also household goods,
Ecover, body care products,
homeopathic remedies and
aromatherapy oils.

Planet Organic

Organic supermarket and veggie cafe

42 Westbourne Grove
(Queensway end)
London W2 5SH

Tel: 020 7727 2227

Open: *Mon-Sat* 9.30–20.30
      Sun 12.00–18.00

Tube: Bayswater

Picnic heaven. Load up here with every kind of veggie food and heaps you never even knew existed. 15 aisles makes this one of the largest retailers of gorgeous organic foods and alcoholic and non-alcoholic drinks, environmentally friendly household goods including Ecover. Not all vegetarian but the non-veggie stuff is right at the back out of sight. No artificial additives in anything, no hydrogenated fat and no refined sugar. Juice and coffee bar. Great book section includes Veggie Guides.

Now a vegetarian hot food bar and salads £2.25–7.00. Eat in or take-away.

Professional health advisors such as nutritionists working here in health and bodycare. Homeopath has a treatment room a couple of days a week.

Portobello Whole Foods

Wholefood shop

Unit 1,2
66 Portobello Road
Ladbroke Grove
London W10 5TY
(Junction with Cambrige Gardens or Acklam Rd, just under the Westway)

Tel: 020-8968 9133

Open: *Mon-Sat* 9.30–18.00
      Sun 11:00–17.00

Tube: Ladbrok Grove

Excellent large wholefood shop in Portobello market area. They pack all their own dry products like nuts, dried fruit, grains and beans, and make their own muesli. Organic fruit and veg. Non-dairy cheeses and ice-cream. Vitamins and supplements. Biodegradable cleaning product, Ecover refills. Small range of toiletries including soaps, toothpastes and moisturisers. There's a Falafel King take-away a few doors down.

Revital

Wholefood shop

Wholefood shop
154 High Street, Hounslow
Middlesex TW3 1LR

Tel: 020-8572-0310

Open: *Mon–Sat* 9.00–17.30,
Sun closed

Tube: Chalk Farm

Wholefood shop, previously called 'Food for thought'– now with a wider range of products; lots of organic food, a wide range of toiletries and cruelty- free cosmetics. They have a take–away section with sandwiches, pies, pasties, salads and burgers, some of which are vegan.

Portobello Market

Market

Portobello Road, W11

Open: *Mon–Sat* 8.00–18.30
not Thur afternoon

Tube: Ladbroke Grove,
Notting Hill Gate

Gigantic market, competing with Walthamstow for the title of longest in Britain, with antiques at the south end, fruit and veg in the middle and clothes and household tat at the top.

VEGETARIAN LONDON
HOT TIPS

Local Groups

Some of these are campaigning groups – these usually have the word "animal". Others are mainly social – look for the word "vegan" or "vegetarian".

Bromley Animal Rights

16 Parkside Avenue,
Bromley BR1 2EJ

Tel: 020-8464 6035

Bromley and Environs Vegetarian Group

For the latest newsletter send A5 sae to
Kathy Silk, BEVEG,
c/o Bronwen Humphreys,
The Vegetarian Society,
Parkdale, Dunham Rd,
Altrincham, Cheshire WA14 4QG.

Or email messages clearly headed BEVEG to
bron@vegsoc.org

Friendly crowd of members get together in the area for coffee mornings or afternoon tea once a month except Jan, Feb & Aug. Exchange ideas, recipes, have cookery books on sale, free leaflets and a bring & buy table to raise funds. Bring a friend on your first visit if you wish. Vegans welcome.

Admission/refreshments 75p.

Bromley Eating Experience

Diana Elvin: Tel: 020 8777 1680
Email: bromleyveg@talk21.com

Events: Meetings on the second Saturday of alternate months from March, 12–3pm. Usually with speaker or video. Bring non-flesh food and soft drinks to share, buffet style. All welcome. Parking on site. Friends MeetingHouse,Ravensbourne Road, Bromley.

Campaign Against Leather& Fur

BM Box 8880, London WC1N 3XX
www.londonveganfestival.org.uk

Organisers of the annual London Vegan Festival. The next one is on Sunday 25th September 2005, 10am–7pm at Kensington Town Hall, Hornton Street W8.

Croydon Vegans

61 Warren Road,
Croydon CR0 6PF.

Tel: 020-8655 3797.
tandj@moosenet.
free-online.co.uk

Campaigning and social events. Fundraising for Animal Aid and other organisations. Regular newsletter.

Croydon Vegetarian Group

Helen Buckland

Tel: 020-8688 6325

Group promoting vegetarianism, with information stalls and events. Offers of help always welcome.

Elmbridge Animal Aid and Compassion in World Farming and Naturewatch

local contact for SW London
Elizabeth Shaw

Tel: 020-8398 4003

Gay Vegetarians and Vegans & Fur

GV, BM 5700, London WC1N 3XX

Meet on first Sunday of each month between 16.00 and 18.00 in a room in the Bryant Street Community Church,

Stratford, London. Write to them to check that they will be meeting.

Vegan Harlow

info@veganharlow.co.uk
www.veganharlow.co.uk

Harrow Vegetarian Society

Mr K Joshi
Tel: 020 8907 1235
Email:kjoshi@pradipsweet.co.uk

Hounslow Vegetarian Information Centre

Pat Buckingham:
Tel: 020 8560 7756;
Email: p.wbuckingham@btopen-world.com

Kingston and Richmond Vegetarians

Martin 020-8541 3437
John 020-8977 9648
martin.h2o@tiscali.co.uk

Vegetarians, vegans and those interested in vegetarianism are welcome to join our small but friendly group. Monthly restaurant visit as well as campaigning and other events.

Leaves of Life

The Advent Centre, Banqueting
Suite, 39 Brendon Street,
London W1
(Corner of Crawford Place)
E-mail leavesoflife@aol.com
www.leavesoflife.org
Tel: 020-8881 8865

This vegan organisation
meets usually once a month
at the above address. They
promote the health aspects
of vegan nutrition. A typical
meeting starts with a
cookery demonstration
followed by a lecture by a
vegan doctor or health practitioner. Topics include
diabetes, osteoporosis,
hydrotherapy, cancer,
arthritis, ulcers, digestive
orders, atherosclerosis and
how a plant based diet
avoids or helps reverse
these. £3 suggested
donation, £1.50 conces-
sions, for food and lecture.
For more details phone or e-
mail.

Lesbian Vegan Group

katiesilvester@hotmail.com
Tel: 020-8523 0882

Meet in vegetarian restaurants and members' houses
for potluck meals where
everyone brings a different
dish. Picnics in summer.
Members from many
countries. Vegetarian and
bisexual women welcome, all
members eat vegan food
while with the group.

London Animal Action

BM 2248, London WC1N 3XX
Meeting address:
Marchmont Community Centre,
62 Marchmont Street,
London WC1.
Tube: Russell Square (Piccadilly
Line, closest), Chancery Lane,
Euston, King's Cross, Euston
Square.
www.laa.org.uk, info@laa.org.uk
Tel: 0845-458 4775 (local rate)

Meetings: 7.30-9.00pm, 2nd
Monday of the month. Vegan
food served afterwards.
Extremely active
campaigning group with
weekly anti-fur demos in
London, minibuses to animal
abusing establishments
around the country, street
stalls, vegan food fayres and
social events. Subscribe
online to monthly newsletter
and read back issues online.

Admission/refreshments
75p.

London Vegans

www.londonvegans.org.uk
020-8931 1904

London Vegans exists to promote veganism in the London area. Various social events, such as monthly meetings, restaurant visits and walks. Also information stalls at a variety of events throughout the year, ranging from small bazaars to large festivals. Details of these and other events in The London Vegans Diary, which is updated frequently. For information on the next London Vegans events see the website or telephone the Info Line on (020) 8931 1904 (24 hours) for updates.

The website includes the free **VegCom accommodation** adverts service if you are seeking or offering a room in a vegan house or flat.

Meetings: 6.30pm, last Wednesday of the month (not December), east of Russell Square underground, entrance through security doors adjacent to 38a, press the bell marked Community Centre.

Telephone enquiries (about London Vegans, or veganism in general):

Julie / Brian: 020-8446 3480

E-mail: Brian and Julie at info@londonvegans.org.uk, type "enquiry" in the subject line.

Paul Halford on 01206-861846

Fax enquiries:
020 8931 1904

Postal enquiries:
7 Deansbrook Road, Edgware, Middlesex HA8 9BE.

Subscriptions (or a request to be e-mailed full diary) subs@londonvegans.org.uk

Or leave message on infoline 020 8931 1904

Press and media *only*
07956 169214 or media@londonvegans.org.uk

Also don't miss Julie and Brian's website: www.veganlondon.co.uk

Muslim Vegan and Vegetarian Society

Rafeeque Ahmed
59 Brey Towers, 136 Adelaide
Rd, London NW3 3JU.
Tel: 020-7483 1742.

Publishes Islam and Vegetarianism book, for £1 post free. Main emphasis is on the vegan side, also raw food, combining, timing and additive free.

SEAR

www.se-ar.org.uk
info@se-ar.org.uk

Meeting on the first Tuesday of the Month at 7.30, Ruskin House, 23 Coombe Road, Croydon, CR0 1BD.

South-East Animal Rights campaigning group.

Vegan Essex

www.veganessex.org
http://essex.veganfestival.org
veganessex@hotmail.com

Meet the first Tuesday of the month at the Brentwood School Sports Hall. Lots of social events. Giant vegan festival around 1st November.

Vegetarian & Vegan Gay Group

www.vvgg.freeserve.co.uk

Information line on
020-7713 9063.

Aimed at gay, lesbian, bisexual, transgender & gay-friendly people and their friends who are or would like to be vegetarian or vegan, for socialising and meeting, support in having events with a vegetarian or vegan theme. Advice and information on being vegetarian and vegan and gay including products, shops, restaurants, accommodation, nutrition, health, latest information, discussions.

The group currently meets about twice a month and almost always meets for an indoor veggie picnic from 18.00 on the last Sunday of each month at London Friend, Kings Cross. The other event can vary depending on the season. During cold weather they tend to visit a vegetarian restaurant on the middle Saturday in the evening. During warm weather an outdoor event such as a picnic on the middle Sunday during the day. Other events have included picnics, walks, marches, discussions, visits to festivals, picnics at people's homes and visits to gay venues.

Vegetarian Cycling and Athletic Club

www.geocities.com/vegetariancac

Running, Peter Simpson
01908-503919, psimpson@vegcac-mkveg.fslife.co.uk

Cycling, Steve Wigglesworth
steve@37thl.freeserve.co.uk

Duathlon/Triathlon, Steve Coote
01582-666243,
che@milliemax.fsworld.co.uk
020-8655 3797.

Vegetarian Social Club

Helen Buckland
Tel: 020-8688 6325
(no media calls please)

Social club based around London. Wide ranging events from theatre visits and meals to walks and days out.

Veggie socials

Rob Lewis. 01234-365651
info@veggiesocials.co.uk
www.veggiesocials.co.uk

Free social group for veggies who can attend events in London and surrounding areas

Young Indian Vegetarians

Nitin Mehta, M.B.E.,
226 London Rd, West Croydon, Surrey CR0 2TE
Tel: 020-8681 8884
animalahimsa@yahoo.co.uk

Active, campaigning group. Welcomes opportunity to give talks, presentations. Various big events around London.

HUNT SABOTEURS

http://hsa.enviroweb.org
BM HSA, London WC1N 3XX
Telephone 0845 4500727

Fancy a different day out in the country until fox hunting finally stops for real? Contact your local hunt sabs and join the national association. If you don't want to risk getting duffed up by hunters and terriermen while the cops stand by and then arrest you and your mates (no kidding), you can always help with street stalls and fund raising. Check the website for local groups around London.

The Nationals

If there's no vegetarian or animal rights group listed near you, contact any of these for the address of your local contact or group. If you want to go veggie or vegan, or know someone who might be interested, they have stacks of literature to help you and can answer questions. If you want to help spread the word and get active for animal rights, they would love to hear from you. And they all have brilliant websites. Always enclose a stamped addressed envelope or a donation.

Animal Aid

www.animalaid.org.uk

The Old Chapel, Bradford St, Tonbridge, Kent TN9 1AW.

Tel: 01732-364 546
Fax: 01732-366 533

£10 waged, £7 unwaged, £5 youth. The experts on U-18 campaigns for all areas of animal rights including vivisection, school dissection, school debates, displays, vegetarianism, veganism, circuses, zoos.

Animal Rights Coalition

http://arcnews.
redblackandgreen.net

PO Box 339,
Wolverhampton WV10 7BZ

Tel: 0845-458 0146

Network of Britain's 500 most active local animal rights groups and grassroots campaigners. For local animal rights news from around the country, subscribe to 12 monthly issues of ARCNews newsletter for £10.

People for the Ethical Treatment of Animals

www.peta.org.uk
See advert page 16.

Realfood

PO Box 339,
Wolverhampton WV10 7BZ

Tel: 0845-458 0146
www.realfood.org.uk

Grassroots campaigning vegan group making it easier for people to follow a vegan diet.

The Vegan Society

www.vegansociety.com
See advert page 11.

The Vegetarian Society

www.vegsoc.org
See advert page 3.

Vegetarian and Vegan Foundation

www.vegetarian.org.uk
See advert page 14.

Veggies, Nottingham

www.veggies.org.uk
Tel: 0845-458 9595

Publishes the Animal Rights Calendar and Animal Contacts Directory, available on line, which lists every veggie and vegan business and animal rights group in the country.

Viva!
(Vegetarians International Voice for Animals)

www.viva.org.uk
See advert page 14.

Food Brought To You

Many of the restaurants in this book do outside catering, and this is indicated in the text. Here are a few suggestions that we've heard are particularly good. If you want a wicked vegan cake for an office or birthday party, call Beatroot (Soho) or Pogo Cafe (East London).

Barty's Creative Catering

Vegetarian & vegan catering service

83 Stanley Gardenens,
Teddington,
Middlesex TW 11 8SY
Tel: 020-8977 9064

Vegetarian and vegan catering service who will cater for any event, weddings parties, and especially charity events and conferences.

Leon's Vegetarian Catering

Vegetarian and vegan catering

www.leonlewis.co.uk
leonsveg@aol.com
132b London Rd, Brentwood,
Essex CM14 4NS
Tel: 01277-218661

Mouthwatering vegetarian and vegan catering, buffets, cookery demonstrations, any event nationwide. Amazing fungus forays in the woods in autumn and late spring, followed by cooking the booty and quaffing from Leon's extensive wine cellar.

Naklank

Vegetarian Indian catering

50b Ealing Road, Wembley,
Middlesex HAO 4TQ
Tel: 020-8902 8008

Indian sweet shop and restaurant catering for parties and weddings.

Veggies Catering Campaign

Vegan catering cooperative

The Sumac Centre
245 Gladstone Street
Nottingham NG7 6HX
Tel: 0845-458 9595

info@veggies.org.uk
www.veggies.org.uk

Part of a large resource centre, Veggies does very low cost veggie and vegan catering nationwide for various events, organisations and charities with burgers, salads, lots of cakes.

Wild Cherry

Vegetarian Buddhist catering

241 Globe Road, Bethnal Green
London E2 0JD
Tel: 020-8980 6678

Vegetarian Buddhist group that run a café and do outside catering.

Organic Delivery Company

Vegetarian grocery delivery service

www.organicdelivery.co.uk
Tel: 020-7739 8181

Not exactly a caterer, but for people with no time to shop they will deliver organic vegetarian groceries, household products, baby food and booze, to your home or office, daytime and evening. Regular orders or one-off deliveries.

Veggie places to stay

Barrow House

Vegetarian bed & breakfast

45 Barrow Road, Streatham
Common, London SW16 5PE

Tel: 020-8677 1925
Fax: 020-8677 1925

Train: Streatham Common
British Rail.
Close to the A23 London to
Brighton road.

Open: All year round

Vegetarian and vegan bed
and breakfast in south
London, in a Victorian family
house in a quiet location, 15
minutes by rail from Victoria
Station.

Three double/twin rooms,
£50 double or £35 single.

Breakfast features fruit salad,
cereal, toast, soya margarine
and milk always available
and even soya yogurt if they
know you're coming.

Two vegetarian restaurants
and a wholefood store
nearby.

Stephanie Rothner

Bed & breakfast

44 Grove Road
North Finchley, London N12 9DY

Tel: 020-8446 1604

Mobile: 07956-406446

Tube: Woodside Park then 15
min walk or Finchely bus
terminal

Open: All year round

Newish vegetarian homely
bed and breakfast, her mum
runs the one in N3.

1 single and 1 double at £16
per person per night
including breakfast. Shared
bathroom. Veggie breakfast
with soya milk and
margarine always available.
Children over twelve only.
No smoking or pets. Two
friendly resident cats. They
don't charge single person
supplement.

Temple Lodge

Vegetarian bed & breakfast

51 Queen Caroline Street
Hammersmith, London W6 9QL

Tel: 020-8748 8388

Fax: 020-8563 2758

Tube: Hammersmith, 5 mins

Open: All year

m.beaumont@rdplus.net

No smoking throughout

Temple Lodge is a quiet oasis in the middle of London. There are four single rooms at £30 per night or £195 per week, and three twin rooms at £50 per room per night or £330 per week, plus two double rooms from £50 per night.

A hearty continental breakfast is served in a light, airy basement dining room. Soya milk and vegan margarine are available on request.

You won't have to walk far for lunch or dinner as The Gate vegetarian restaurant is on the same premises. (closed Sunday)There is also a vegetarian Indian restaurant Sagar at 157 King Street and the new vegan restaurant 222 at 222 North End Road.

Visitors are invited to join in with the activities of the Christian Community and will have opportunity of joining the Temple Lodge Club for a nominal fee. The house offers many facilities for the use of guests, such as a kitchen, a quiet and secluded garden and a large library.

The house is thought to be built on the foundations of a seventeenth century building. The artist Sir Frank Brangwyn lived there during the early part of the twentieth century, and both house and grounds have been restored to their former glory.

All major tourist attractions are reached easily by public transport. Pleasant walks along the River Thames are easily accessible. Historical houses, Kew Gardens, the Waterfowl sanctuary of the Wetlands Centre and three theatres are all within walking distance. Close to Olympia and Earls Court Exhibition Centres.

Washbasins are in the rooms, and hairdryers are available on request.

Veggie places to stay (continued)

The Violin B&B

Vegetarian bed & breakfast

24 The Dee, Grovehill
Hemel Hempstead
Hertfordshire HP2 6EN
Tel: 020-01442-388977
Train: Hemel Hempstead 3 miles
Open: All year round
contact@theviolinbnb.co.uk
www.theviolinbnb.co.uk

Vegetarian, homestyle B&B based in Hemel Hempstead. 20 miles from London, conveniently close to the M1 and M25. There is a rail link with Euston station and a very economical Green line Bus service almost every hour into central London.

R£25 per person per night, £30 for single occupancy, including continental breakfast with a shot of hand juiced bio-dynamic wheat-grass juice. Discounted rate for 7+ nights.

A tasty 3 course evening meal may be available if booked in advance for £10. Food is vegetarian or vegan, organic where possible.

Toiletries contain no animal products and are cruelty-free. Broadband internet available.

By train: we are situated three miles from Hemel Hempstead Station, which is on the main line from Birmingham to London Euston. To see a timetable click here

By air: We are only 10 miles from Luton Airport and 22 miles from Heathrow. We can collect or deliver you to either airport. £15 for Luton, £25 for Heathrow, any time of day/night. We're still waiting for planning permission for a Heli-pad in the back garden...

We look forward to meeting you.

HAMPSTEAD VILLAGE GUESTHOUSE
2 Kemplay Road, Hampstead
London NW3 1SY

www.hampsteadguesthouse.com
tel: +44 (0)20 7435 8679   **Fax:** +44 (0)20 7794 0254
e-mail: info@hampsteadguesthouse.com

- Peaceful setting, close to Hampstead Heath, yet in the heart of lively Hampstead Village.

- Close to underground and bus. Centre of London in 10 minutes.

- Large rooms full of character, plus modern amenities: TV, kettle and direct-dial telephone.

- breakfast in the garden, weather permitting.

- Accomodation from £48.

- No smoking.

"If you're looking for something a little different, make a beeline for Annemarie van der Meer's Hampstead home."
Chosen as one of the "Hotels of the Year". The Which? Hotel Guide 2000.

Veggie–friendly places to stay

Dora Rothner

Bed and Breakfast

23 The Ridgeway
Finchley, London N3 2PG
Tel: 020-8346 0246
Tube: Finchley Central
Open: All year round

Homely bed and breakfast in North London, where they're used to doing vegetarian or vegan breakfasts as Dora the owner doesn't eat meat. 2 doubles (not twins) and 1 ingle for £18 per person per night, including breakfast. TV in rooms. Shared bathroom.

Soya milk and margarine always available. No smoking or pets and only children over twelve. Handy for Finchley Central tube (Northern line), the North Circular Road and M1. Rani Indian vegetarian restaurant close by. They are open all year round including at Christmas and don't charge a single person supplement.

Hampstead Village Guesthouse

Veggie friendly hotel

2 Kemplay Road
Hampstead, London NW3 1SY
Tel: 020-7435 8679
Fax: 020-7794 0254
Tube: Hampstead
Parking can be arranged.
Open: All year round
www.HampsteadGuesthouse.com
info@HampsteadGuesthouse.com

Veggie friendly 1872 Victorian guest house in a peaceful setting close to the heath and tube. In the heart of lively Hampstead Village, a fun area with art cinema, restaurants with veggie food, coffee shops and pubs. The large, very comfortable rooms are full of character with sitting area, writing desk, remote control TV, hairdryer, iron, fridge (brilliant for veggies), kettle, telephone, books and even a hot-waterbottle to cuddle.

En suite double £84, en suite single £66. Double £72, singles £48 and £54. Large studio with kitchen and shower £90 for 1, £120 for

2, £138 for 3, £150 for 4, £162 for 5. Parking £10 per day.

Optional breakfast £7 from 8.00 a.m., 9.00 at weekends until late, can be in the garden in summer and you can invite guests.

Booking requires credit card, pay on arrival in cash, sterling (travellers) cheques or credit card (5% surcharge). No smoking in house. No meals except breakfast, but there are veggie restaurants and a wholefood store in the area and veggie dishes in other nearby restaurants.

Liz Heavenstone's

Apartment

Liz Heavenstone's Guest House
192 Regents Park Road
Hampstead, London NW1 8XP

Tel: 020-7722 7139

Fax: 020-7586 3004

Tube: Chalk Farm

Open: All year

lizheavenstone@onetel.com

___

Cosy, top floor apartment in a Regency terrace in Primrose Hill village, on the edge of Regent's Park. Two double/twin rooms, £55-65 per room per night, one with own bathroom, one with shower, which become a self contained apartment with living room when both rooms are taken. There's also a futon for an extra bed in one room. Good for self-catering as the kitchen-breakfast room has fridge, dishwasher, cooker, and microwave-cum-oven.

Add £5 for self-service vegetarian organic breakfast, which can easily be veganized, and they'll happily cater for special diets if you tell them in advance. There are always tea, coffee and herbal drinks, and the breakfast room has a bowl of fruit.

Children welcome but no pets. They have plenty of info on London for guests. Good location, close to the centre but not in the centre. Nearby are Triyoga Centre (www.triyoga.co.uk), which has drop-in classes and the Little Earth veggie cafe, Primrose Hill, Regents Park, Manna vegetarian restaurant, Cafe Seventy Nine and Sesame wholefood store. Camden is a short walk away. Two minutes walk to Chalk Farm underground. Prior telephone booking is essential, do not just turn up.

Veggie–friendly places to stay

(continued)

Mount View

Vegetarian friendly guest house

31 Mount View Road
London N4 4SS

Tel: 020-8340 9222
Fax: 020-8342 8494
Tube: Finsbury Park & W7 bus
Open: All year round

www.mountviewguesthouse.com
MountViewBB@aol.com

Smart Victorian house with garden in a quieter area of North London, combining tranquility and the gentle pace of village life but within easy reach of central London. A quiet haven after a busy day sightseeing. Rooms decorated using natural materials.

Double en suite with sofa in bay window and antique furniture £35 per person. Double £25 per person. Twin with shower £27.50. Single £40–45. 10% discount for 7+ nights.

Vegetarian breakfast available. Vegan and other diets on request.

No evening meal, but Haelan Centre health food store is nearby and Jai Krishna vegetarian restaurant. There are plenty more vegetarian restaurant on the Victoria and Piccadilly underground lines which go right through central London.

15 minutes walking from Finsbury Park tube and rail station, luggage can be collected when you arrive.

Near Highgate cemetery, Hampstead Heath with Kenwood House, Alexandra Palace.

All rooms with tv, hairdryer, washbasin, tea and coffee making facilities. Washing machine and dryer and internet access available on request. Payphone.

Unrestricted parking in street. No smoking throughout. No pets. Children welcome but no high chair. Dutch and French spoken. MC, Visa

AA 5 diamonds.

The Lanesborough

Luxury hotel

Hyde Park Corner, Knightsbridge
London SW1X 7TA

Tel: 020-7259 5599

Fax: 020-7259 5606

For reservations in USA call
toll free 1-800 999 1828
fax: 1-800 937 8278

Tube: Hyde Park Corner

Open: All Year Round

www.lanesborough.com

Luxury hotel popular with veggie rock and movie stars and C.E.O.'s. Singles £285, doubles £395 up to the royal suite for £5000, all plus VAT.

If a veggie/vegan breakfast is required you have to give prior notice at the time of booking. Services include 24 hour butler, fitness centre, spa studio, business centre, complimentary internet access in your room with on-demand film.

The in-house restaurant The Conservatory features gourmet vegetarian dinners, prepared by top chef Paul Gayler or one of his brigade of 40 chefs. Lunch is £24 for 2 courses or £27.50 for three, dinner prices depend on the day of the week but usually range from £32-£44 per head. The vegetarian a la carte menu often has vegan options but not always so phone ahead. There is live music every night and dancing on Friday and Saturday nights.

Moving to London

If you're moving to London for at least six months, then an apartment (flat) with friends can be cheaper than a hostel and much quieter. And much nicer too if you share a kitchen with veggies. Finding an apartment is a full time job for a few days but it can be done if you're persistent.

A single or double room in a houseshare will be £70-120 per week, a studio flat £100 per week and up. You'll need a month's deposit, a month's rent up front, and the contract will normally be a six months assured shorthold tenancy. Staying in a hostel for the first weeks is a lot less hassle while you find a job and you can get some mates there, or go to vegetarian and vegan events to find new friends. (page 230)

A word of warning: London is expensive. The majority of people work hard so they can afford to enjoy it to the full, but live in a small space, probably just one or maybe two rooms. People who turn up wanting to move in with them without paying rent create awkwardness and embarrassment all round. So before coming, make sure you have plenty of money to tide you over for a few weeks while you find a job.

LOOT

London's free ads newspaper

www.loot.com

If you want to rent a whole apartment, this is the place. Buy an early bird token on line to see all the latest ads, of just browse to get a feel for prices. You can place a free ad yourself and let the landlords come to you. Search on "veg" to find veggie houseshares. A printed version of LOOT can be bought in newsagents.

VegCom

Veggie accommodation adverts

www.vegcom.org.uk
or www.veganlondon.org.uk
and click on VegCom

Vegans and veggies looking for flatmates.

Generator Hostel

The king of hostels, fab location

Compton Place,
behind 37 Tavistock Place,
London WC1H 9SD

Tel: 020-7388 7666

Fax: 020-7388 7666

Tube: Russell Square,
Kings Cross, Euston

Open: All year, 24 hours

info@the-generator.co.uk
www.the-generator.co.uk

International 837 bed hostel in Bloomsbury. The cheapest dorms you have to wait for, so you'll probably pay £17 for a 4-bed room. Nearby are Vegetarian Paradise restaurant and Alara Wholefoods (where vegans can buy breakfast). Age 18-35, but older young-at-hearts welcome. Busy bar. Bring earplugs and a padlock for your locker. Towels provided.

Other Hostels

Rock bottom accommodation

www.piccadillyhotel.net
www.astorhostels.com
www.st-christophers.co.uk
www.yhalondon.org.uk
www.ukhostels.com
www.totalhostels.com

Our favourite guidebooks for budget places are *Lonely Planet, Rough Guides* or *Let's Go London, England, Britain* or *Europe*. Off season you can often just turn up, but at weekends and in summer you absolutely must reserve ahead for your first night.

If you've just got off a coach or airport train at Victoria station, there are some accommodation agencies that can sort out your first night's stay for a small commission.

Camping

Crystal Palace Campsite

Bed & breakfast

Crystal Palace Parade,
London SE19
Tel: 020-020-8778 7155
Fax: 020-
Train: Crystal Palace BR
Open: All year round

This is a caravan park so electricity is available but no shop or cooking facilities. They do have laundry and washing facilities though. Rates vary according to the time of year. Average is £2.50 per tent, then £3.75 per adult in winter rising to £4.50 adult in summer. Car and tent is £3.50.

Lee Valley Park

Bed & breakfast

Pickets Lock Centre, London N9
Tel: 020-020-8803 6900
Tube: Tottenham Hale,
Edmonton BR
Open: All Year except Xmas Day,
Boxing Day & New Year

Huge well equipped site set in 6 acres with sports centre and leisure complex with 12 screen cinema, swimming pool, golf course, kids' play area, 3 pubs and pizza restaurant. Acts as bus terminal for those going into town. There is a minimum charge for everyone £5.65 for adult or £2.35 for children 5-16, for individuals this goes up to £8.00 (i.e. one person and tent). Electricity is £2.40 per night. No charge for dogs or awnings. Another site is nearby at Sewardstone Road, Chingford, E4 7RA Tel 020-8529 5689, closed in winter.

Tent City Acton

Bed & breakfast

Old Oak Common Lane, Acton, London W3
Tel: 020-8743 5708
Tube: East Acton
Open: May –Oct 24 hours

Bunk beds in large dorm tents, or bring your own. Prices start at £6 per person. Showers, toilets, basic snack bar.

Tent City Hackney

Bed & breakfast

Millfields Road, Hackney,
London E5 0AR

Tel: 020–8985 7656

Fax: 020–8985 7656

Tube: No. 38 bus to
Clapton Pond

Open: May– October

---

3 large dormitories in tents
with bunk beds. Separate
and mixed dorms. Prices
start around £5 per person,
Under 5's free. Snack bar
with salad, sandwiches and
fruit open 8–12.00 then
19.00–22.00. Free cooking
facilities, on site entertain-
ment, free hot showers,
laundry, valuables lock-up,
no curfew. Canalside pubs
nearby. Profits go to charity.

Days Out of London

Here are some fabulous central veggie places to eat out when you take a trip outside London. For hundreds more, pick up a copy of *Vegetarian Britain* or, for Paris, *Vegetarian Europe*.

Bath

De Muths

Vegetarian restaurant

2 North Parade Passage,
off Abbey Green, Bath, BA1 1NX
Tel: 01225–446 059
Open: Every day 10.00–22.00
Fri–Sat till 23.00,
Sat from 09.00),
Closed daily 17.30–18.00
www.demuths.co.uk

Vegetarian dishes from all around the world, half of them vegan. Menus change every months.

12 entrées £2.75–4.95 such as soup, hummus, guacamole, roasted squash and pumpkin, nachos. Fabulous main courses £5.95–8.50 day, £11.75 evening. Vegans will think they've landed in dessert heaven.

House wine £11.75 a bottle or £3.15 a glass.

The Porter

Vegetarian pub

15 George Street
Bath, BA1 2EN
Tel: 01225–424104
Open: All year round
www.theporter.co.uk

Much of the food is under £5 and includes traditional pub grub and a varied menu, half of it vegan. Cashew nut curry, ratatouille, Trinidadian casserole and homemade soup. Veggie Sunday roast.

Some ciders and beers are vegetarian. Small glass of wine £2.80, large £3.95, bottles 11–£12.80. Beer £2.50–£2.90 for a bottle.

Mon–Thu evening they have live music. DJs Fri and Sat. Sun night is comedy cavern.

Brighton

Foor For Friends

Vegetarian restaurant and cafe

17-18 Prince Albert Street,
Brighton, East Sussex, BN1 1HF
Tel: 01273-202310
Open: Mon-Sat 11.30-22.00
Sun 11.30-22.00

Soup and bread £2.35, medium salad £3.90, hot dishes £4.95-£6.95. Gluten free and nut free diets catered for.

Cocktails, organic and vegan wines.

Terre a Terre

Gourmet vegetarian restaurant

71 East Stree, Brighton BN1 1HQ
Tel: 01273-729051
Open: Tue 18.00-22.30
Wed-Fri 12.00-15.00,
18.00-22.30
Sat-Sun 12.00-22.30
www.terreaterre.co.uk

You'll feel truly spoilt here with dishes from many countries. Book early for evening meals, especially at weekends.

Starters £4.95-6.40, or share Terre a Tapas for two people

for £14. Six salads £6.20 or £10.80 as a main. Eight main courses £10.80-£11.80. Nine desserts £4.50-5.50 including vegan truffles.

Organic veggie and vegan wine list, beers and coffee. Kid's portions.

Bristol

Cafe Maitreya

Vegetarian restaurant

89 St Mark's Road, Easton
Bristol BS5 6HY (near M32)
Tel: 0117-951 0100
Open: Very complicated opening hours. Basically closed Mon all day and Tue lunchtime.
www.cafemaitreya.co.uk
thesnug@cafemaitreya.co.uk

Bristol at last has a really excellent veggie restaurant with lots for vegans.

Weekend cooked breakfast £5.25-5.95. Lunch dishes from £3.50, mezze £5.95.

Evening two courses £12.45, three £15.95. Amazing desserts. Juices and smoothies. Vegan wines, beers and ciders.

Days Out (continued)

Cambridge

Rainbow Bistro

Vegetarian restaurant

9A Kings Parade,
Cambridge CB2 1SJ

Tel: 01223-321551

Open: Tue-Sat 10.00-22.00
(last orders 21.30)
Sun-Mon closed

www.rainbowcafe.co.uk

Popular with local vegans and visitors. Soup £2.95, mains £7.25.

All cakes home made, half vegan, £3.75. Vegan ice-cream.

Vegan organic wine, beer and cider.

Children's dishes £3.25 such as risotto, pasta and small versions of the mains.

Oxford

The Garden

Veggie meals in traditional pub

at The Gardeners Arms pub
Plantation Road,
Jericho, Oxford

Tel: 01865-559814

Open: Wed- Fri 12.00-15.00,
17.00-21.00
Sat 12.00-21.00
Sun 12.00-18.00

www.thegardenoxford.co.uk

Pub with only veggie and vegan food.

Snacks £2-£3.95 such as ciabatta or sausage with fries.

Ciabatta sandwiches £4.95 with side salad. Burgers with fries £5.65. Salads and nine mains £4.95-£5.95 such as Thai green curry, vegan vegetable korma and pasta dishes.

Paris

Le Potager du Marais

Vegetarian restaurant

22 Rue Rambuteau,
3rd arrondissement
Tel: 01-42 74 24 66
Metro: Rambuteau (line 11),
Hotel de Ville (1 and 11)

Open: Mon-Sat 12-24.00
Sun 13-24.00
last orders 22.30

It's only three hours to Paris by train from Waterloo, and there are lots of vegetarian restaurants there in *Vegetarian Europe*. This is a new one, the first to open in the central 3rd arrondissement, next to the Pompidou Centre, and it's been getting rave reviews from French vegetarians and vegans. Dishes from 7 to 12.50 euros or a set menu for 15 euros. Separate vegan page in its menu. Smoking allowed.

Your Hot Tips

Make a note here of any new places in London from the Veggie Guides update page:

www.vegetarianguides.co.uk/updates

VEGETARIAN LONDON
INDEXES

Eat Vegan	Eat organic	Eat cheap	Eat posh
Drink & Eat veggie	Have coffee & tea	Have a veggie breakfast	Take kids

Care and feeding of your vegan: he or she will purr with delight at superb buffets, vegan cakes, desserts and soya ice-cream.

Central

Beatroot	24
Chi	42
Country Life	28
CTB	85
Fresh & Wild, Soho	30
Health Food Centre	54
Joi	76
Maoz	33
Neal's Yard Salad Bar	40
Planet Organic, Tott Ct Rd	75
Pure	83
Rye Wholefoods	87
Tai Buffet, Gt Chapel St	33
Tai, Greek St	31
Wai	76
London Vegans	233

North

CTV, Golders Green	119
Friendly Falafels	122
Little Earth Café	102
Manna	101
Organic13	124
Peking Palace	128
Pita	119
Rasa, Stoke Newington	94
Tai Buffet, Camden	111
Tai Buffet, Islington	116
Tai Buffet, Muswell Hill	133

Tai Noodle Bar, Camden	110
Tony's Natural Foods	115
VitaOrganic	121

East

Pogo Café	149

South

Cicero's	161
Domali	175
Pepperton UK	173
Pushkar, Café	165
Riverside Vegetaria	182
Service Heart Joy	170
Shahee Bhelpoori	172
Veggie One	183
Wholemeal Café	174

West

222	197
Chai	213
Fresh & Wild, Westbourne Gr	222
Gate, The	196
Luscious Organic	225
Planet Organic, Fulham	193
Planet Organic, Westbourne Gr	226

Specialists in organic meals, snacks, provisions, fruit and vegetables.

Central

Country Life	28
Fresh & Wild, Soho	30
Fresh & Wild, City	88
Neal's Yard Bakery	39
Planet Organic, Tott Ct Rd	75

North

Fresh & Wild, Camden	106
Fresh & Wild, N16	95
Heartstone	106
Little Earth Café	102
Manna	101
Organic13	124
VitaOrganic	121

East

Spitalfields Market, Sunday	151

South

Fresh & Wild, Clapham	163
Tide Tables	184

West

Fresh & Wild, Westbourne Gr	222
Hugo's	209
Luscious Organic	225
Organic Café, Chelsea	190
Planet Organic, Fulham	193
Planet Organic, Westbourne Gr	226

All-you-can-eat bargain buffets, student favourites, big portions at low prices.

Central

North

East

South

West

Elegance, gourmet grub and perhaps candles for a romantic soiree or important client.

Central

North

East

South

West

| Eat Vegan | Eat organic | Eat cheap | Eat posh |
| Drink & Eat veggie | Have coffee & tea | Have a veggie breakfast | Take kids |

Quaff while you scoff at these licensed eateries, or bring your own (BYO) from the nearby offie.

Central

North

East

| Eat posh | Eat cheap | Eat organic | Eat vegan |
| Take kids | Have a veggie breakfast | Have coffee & tea | Drink & Eat veggie |

South

West

eat Vegan	Eat organic	Eat cheap	Eat posh
Drink & Eat veggie	Have coffee & tea	Have a veggie breakfast	Take kids

Favourite chill out spots for sipping tea, (soya) cappuccino, latte, nibbling cake.

Central

Alara	48
Bean Juice	72
Beatroot	24
Carrie Awaze	42
Casse-Croute	62
Coffee Matters	50
Coopers	60
Country Life	28
Falafel Cafes, Leicester Sq	34
First Out	43
Food for Thought	38
Fresh & Wild Soho	30
Gaby's	33
Govinda's	26
Greenery, The	84
LSE Café	43
Maoz	33
Mary Ward	49
Meze Café	57
Neal's Yard Bakery	39
Neal's Yard Salad Bar	40
Place Below, The	81
Planet Organic, Tottenham Ct Rd	75
Red Veg	31
Rye Wholefoods	87
Tiffin Bites, Cannon St	86
Tiffin Bites, Liverpool St	86
Tiffin Bites, Moorgate	86
Wheatley's	84
Woolley's	50
World Food Café	41

North

Bliss Patisserie	117
Candid Café	116
Dream Temple	105
Fresh & Wild, Camden	106
Fresh & Wild, N16	95
Greenhouse, The	139
Healthier Eating Café	109
Higher Taste	97
Jiva Juice	105
Little Earth Café	102
Organic13	124
Phoenicia	125
Pilgrims	96
Pita	119
Queens Wood Café	127
Seventy Nine, Café	103
Taboon Bakery	120
Tony's Natural Foods	115
Tupelo Honey	110
Veggie House	134

East

West

South

Eat Vegan	Eat organic	Eat cheap	Eat posh
Drink & Eat veggie	Have coffee & tea	**Have a veggie breakfast**	Take kids

Open early for a bowl of muesli or full English cooked veggie breakfast.

Central

North

East

South

West

These places welcome the little darlings with high chairs, children's portions or special menus.

Central

Carnevale	80
Country Life	28
Govinda's	26
Mildred's	27
Neal's Yard Salad Bar	40
Place Below, The	81
Rasa, Oxford St	71
Tas, Waterloo	61

North

Healthier Eating Café	109
Little Earth Café	102
Manna	101
Organic13	124
Peking Palace	128
Queens Wood Café	127

East

Chawalla	152
Crown, The (pub)	146
Gallery Café	146
Pogo Café	149
Ronak Restaurant	152
Wild Cherry	144

South

Cicero's	161
Green Café	185
Hollyhock Café	185
Kastoori	169
Pushkar, Café	165
Riverside Vegetaria	182
Santok Maa's	185
Shahee Bhelpoori	172
Swad	186
Tide Tables	184
Wholemeal Café	174

West

Chai	213
Chetna's	201
Garden Café	220
Gate, The	196
Hugo's	209
Jashan	202
Jays Pure	214
Kalamaras	220
Kathiyawadi	218
Maru's Bhajia House	203
Pradip	216
Ram's	216
Rose	215
Sabras	208
Sagar	198
Sarashwathy Bavans	205
Saravanas	210
Shahanshah	219
Swadisht	217
Woodlands, Wembley	206

Restaurants A–Z

Shops A–Z
Take away
Market & street stalls

Restaurants A–Z

Shops A–Z
Take away
Markets & street stalls

V

W

Y

H

Holland & Barrett

J

K

T

U

V

W

H

I

J

K

L

M

N

O

P

R

Restaurants A–Z
Shops A–Z
Take away
Markets & street stalls